everyday
Phonics
Intervention Activities

Table of Contents

Using Everyday Phonics Intervention Activities

Current research identifies phonemic awareness and phonics as the essential skills for reading success.

- **Phonemic awareness** is the ability to notice, think about, and work with the individual sounds in spoken words. Before children learn to read print, they need to become aware of how the sounds in words work. They must understand that words are made up of speech sounds, or phonemes.

- **Phonics** instruction teaches children the relationships between the letters (graphemes) of written language and the individual sounds (phonemes) of spoken language. Children learn to use the relationships to read and write words. Knowing the relationships will help children recognize familiar words accurately and automatically, and "decode" new words.

Although some students master these skills easily during regular classroom instruction, many others need additional re-teaching opportunities to master these essential skills. The Everyday Phonics Intervention Activities series provides easy-to-use, five-day intervention units for Grades K–5. These units are structured around a research-based Model-Guide-Practice-Apply approach. You can use these activities in a variety of intervention models, including Response to Intervention (RTI).

Everyday Phonics Intervention Activities Series Skills	K
Phonemic Awareness	✔
Letter Identificaton and Formation	✔
Sound/Symbol Relationships	✔

Getting Started

In just five simple steps, Everyday Phonics Intervention Activities provides everything you need to identify students' phonetic needs and to provide targeted intervention.

1. PRE-ASSESS to identify students' comprehension needs.

Use the pre-assessment on the CD-ROM to identify the strategies your students need to master.

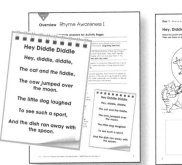

2. MODEL the strategy.

Every five-day unit targets a specific strategy. On Day 1, use the teacher prompts and reproducible activity to introduce and model the strategy.

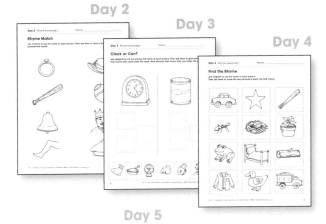

3. GUIDE PRACTICE and APPLY.

Use the reproducible practice activities for Days 2, 3, and 4 to build students' understanding of, and proficiency with, the strategy.

4. MONITOR progress.

Administer the Day 5 reproducible assessment to monitor each student's progress and to make instructional decisions.

5. POST-ASSESS to document student progress.

Use the post-assessment on the CD-ROM to measure students' progress as a result of your interventions.

Using Everyday Intervention for RTI

According to the National Center on Response to Intervention, RTI "integrates assessment and intervention within a multi-level prevention system to maximize student achievement and to reduce behavior problems." This model of instruction and assessment allows schools to identify at-risk students, monitor their progress, provide research-proven interventions, and "adjust the intensity and nature of those interventions depending on a student's responsiveness."

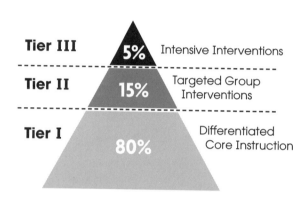

RTI models vary from district to district, but the most prevalent model is a three-tiered approach to instruction and assessment.

The Three Tiers of RTI	Using Everyday Intervention Activities
Tier I: Differentiated Core Instruction • Designed for all students • Preventive, proactive, standards-aligned instruction • Whole- and small-group differentiated instruction • Ninety-minute, daily core reading instruction in the five essential skill areas: phonics, phonemic awareness, comprehension, vocabulary, fluency	• Use whole-group comprehension mini-lessons to introduce and guide practice with comprehension strategies that all students need to learn. • Use any or all of the units in the order that supports your core instructional program.
Tier II: Targeted Group Interventions • For at-risk students • Provide thirty minutes of daily instruction beyond the ninety-minute Tier I core reading instruction • Instruction is conducted in small groups of three to five students with similar needs	• Select units based on your students' areas of need (the pre-assessment can help you identify these). • Use the units as week-long, small-group mini-lessons.
Tier III: Intensive Interventions • For high-risk students experiencing considerable difficulty in reading • Provide up to sixty minutes of additional intensive intervention each day in addition to the ninety-minute Tier I core reading instruction • More intense and explicit instruction • Instruction conducted individually or with smaller groups of one to three students with similar needs	• Select units based on your students' areas of need. • Use the units as one component of an intensive comprehension intervention program.

Everyday Phonics Intervention Activities Grade K • ©2010 Newmark Learning, LLC

Overview Rhyme Awareness I

Directions and Sample Answers for Activity Pages

Day 1	See "Model the Skill" below.
Day 2	Read aloud the title and directions. Invite students to name the pictures in both columns. Then help them match the pictures that rhyme. (**ring/king; bat/hat; bell/shell; leg/egg**)
Day 3	Read aloud the title and directions. Point out the clock and can at the top of each column. Invite students to cut out the pictures and name them. Help them identify which pictures rhyme with **clock** and which rhyme with can and glue them in the correct column. (**Clock: sock, rock, lock. Can: pan, fan, man**)
Day 4	Read aloud the title and directions. Invite students to name the three pictures in each row. Help them identify the two pictures that rhyme and draw a circle around them. (**car/star; ant/plant; frog/log; duck/truck**)
Day 5	Read aloud the directions and name the pictures together. Allow time for students to complete the first task. Then point out the picture of the pan and ask students to draw something that rhymes with **pan**. Afterward, meet individually with students to discuss their results. Use their responses to plan further instruction and review.

Model the Skill

◆ Hand out the Day 1 activity page. Chant the nursery rhyme "Hey Diddle Diddle." Tell students that the nursery rhyme has several rhymes, or words that sound alike at the end. Read the nursery rhyme again, inviting students to listen for the rhymes.

◆ **Say:** *The word **diddle** rhymes with the word **fiddle**. What other rhymes did you hear? Color in the two things that rhyme.* Repeat the nursery rhyme if necessary, then allow time for students to color in the moon and the spoon.

◆ Have students point to the picture of the cat. **Say:** *What rhymes with **cat**? Draw a picture of something that rhymes with **cat**.* After students complete their drawings, have them share with a partner by saying the two words aloud, such as **cat** and **hat**.

Hey Diddle Diddle

Hey, diddle, diddle,

The cat and the fiddle,

The cow jumped over the moon.

The little dog laughed

To see such a sport,

And the dish ran away with the spoon.

Hey, Diddle, Diddle

**Read the poem aloud to students. Ask them to color in the things that rhyme.
Then ask them to draw something below that rhymes with *cat*.**

Hey, diddle, diddle,

The cat and the fiddle,

The cow jumped over the moon.

The little dog laughed

To see such a sport,

And the dish ran away
with the spoon.

Name _____

Rhyme Match

Ask students to say the name of each picture. Then ask them to draw a line to match the pictures that rhyme.

Clock or Can?

Ask students to cut out and say the name of each picture. Then ask them to glue pictures that rhyme with *clock* under the clock. Glue pictures that rhyme with *can* under the can.

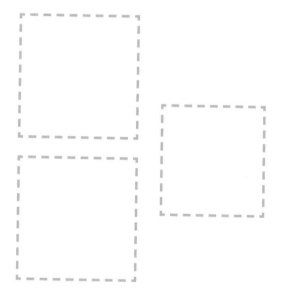

Name _____

Find the Rhyme

Ask students to say the name of each picture.
Then ask them to circle the two pictures in each row that rhyme.

 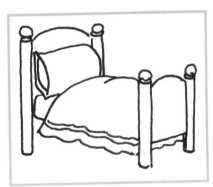 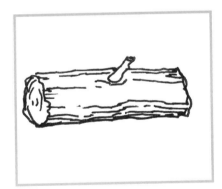

Assessment

Ask students to say the name of the pictures in each pair. If the pictures rhyme, ask them to make a check on the line. If they don't rhyme, make an X.

 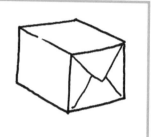    

_____   _____

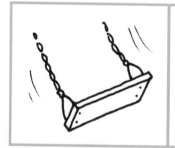     

_____   _____

_____

Ask students to say the name of the picture and to draw something that rhymes with it.

Overview Rhyme Awareness II

Directions and Sample Answers for Activity Pages

Day 1	See "Model the Skill" below.
Day 2	Read aloud the title and directions. Invite students to name the pictures. Then help them cut out the pictures and glue the matching rhymes side by side. (**tree/key; rake/snake; tie/pie**)
Day 3	Read aloud the title and directions. Invite students to name the pictures and draw something that rhymes with each.
Day 4	Pair up students to play the game. Have pairs cut out and shuffle the picture cards. Each player takes three cards, and places the rest of the deck face down. Players take turns asking each other for cards that rhyme. For example, the first player asks, "Do you have a card that rhymes with *bee*?" If the second player has a rhyming picture card, he or she gives it to the first player. If not, the second player says *Go Fish*. The first player draws from the pile to try and make a match. The player with the most matches at the end of the game wins. (**pie/fly; pail/sail; cane/chain; bee/knee; skate/gate; wheel/peel; bone/cone; globe/robe**)
Day 5	Read aloud the directions and name the pictures together. Allow time for students to complete the first task. Then point out the picture of the cake and ask students to draw something that rhymes with **cake**. Afterward, meet individually with students to discuss their results. Use their responses to plan further instruction and review.

Model the Skill

◆ Hand out the Day 1 activity page. Chant the nursery rhyme "It's Raining, It's Pouring." Tell students that the nursery rhyme includes several rhymes, or words that sound alike at the end. Read the nursery rhyme again, inviting students to listen for the rhymes.

◆ **Say:** *The word **pouring** rhymes with the word **snoring**. What other rhymes did you hear? Color in the two things that rhyme.* Repeat the nursery rhyme if necessary, then allow time for students to color in the **head** and the **bed**.

◆ Have students point to the picture of the man. **Say:** *What rhymes with **man**? Draw a picture of something that rhymes with **man**.* After students complete their drawings, have them share with a partner by saying the two words aloud, such as **man** and **fan**.

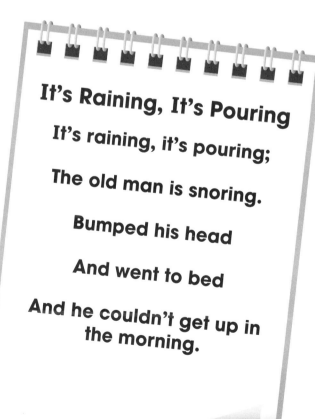

It's Raining, It's Pouring

It's raining, it's pouring;

The old man is snoring.

Bumped his head

And went to bed

And he couldn't get up in the morning.

It's Raining, It's Pouring

Read the poem aloud to students. Ask them to color in the things that rhyme.
Then ask them to draw something that rhymes with *man*.

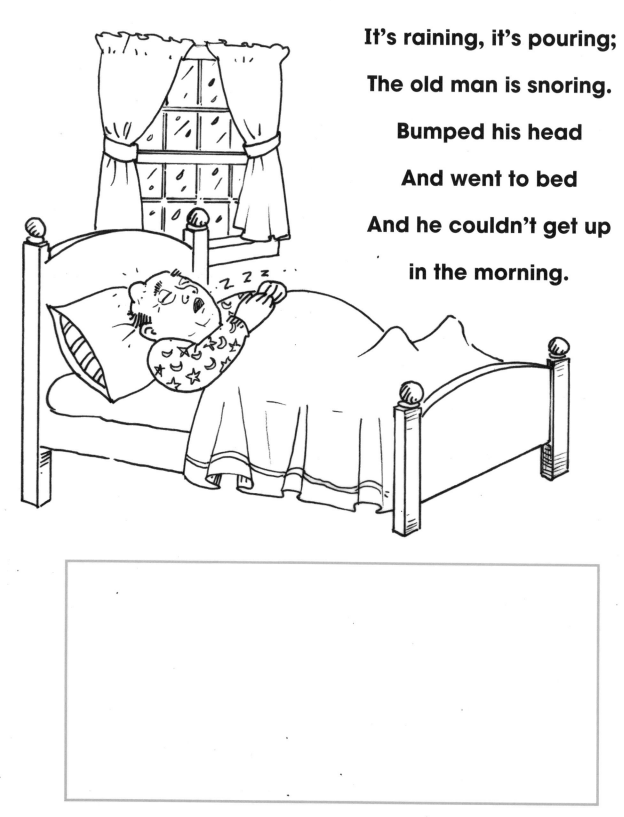

It's raining, it's pouring;

The old man is snoring.

Bumped his head

And went to bed

And he couldn't get up

in the morning.

Name _____

Rhyming Words

Ask students to say the name of each picture. Then ask them to cut out the pictures and glue the rhyming pairs together in the boxes.

Draw a Rhyme

Ask students to say the name of each picture and then draw a picture that rhymes with it.

Go Fish!

Ask student pairs to cut out the pictures and use them to play a rhyme-matching game.

Assessment

Ask students to say the name of the pictures in each pair. If the pictures rhyme, ask them to make a check on the line. If they don't rhyme, make an X.

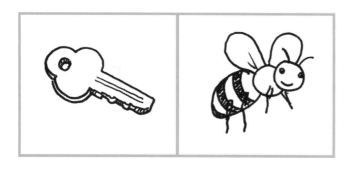

_____   _____

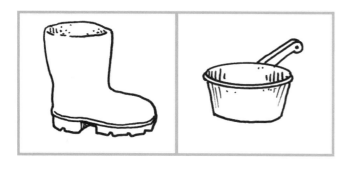

_____   _____

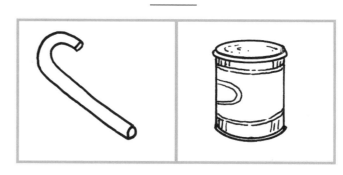

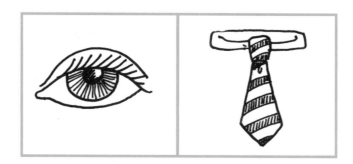

_____

Ask students to say the name of the picture and to draw something that rhymes with it.

Overview Segmenting Words by Syllable

Directions and Sample Answers for Activity Pages

Day 1	See "Model the Skill" below.
Day 2	Read aloud the title and directions. Have students name each picture. Then help students identify and color the pictures with one syllable. (**house, fish, tree, foot**)
Day 3	Read aloud the title and directions. Invite students to name each picture and clap the syllables. Then help them identify the pictures with one syllable and those with two syllables. (One syllable: **kite, ball, frog, hat**. Two syllables: **flower, camel, mitten, pumpkin, rainbow**.)
Day 4	Read aloud the title and directions. After students cut out the picture cards, invite them to name each picture and clap the syllables. Then help them sort the pictures by number of syllables. (One syllable: **pig, cup**. Two syllables: **flashlight, rabbit**. Three syllables: **triangle, banana**.)
Day 5	Read aloud the directions and name the pictures together. Allow time for students to complete the first task. Then say the words **baby** and **lamp** and ask students to tally or write the number of syllables they hear in each word. Afterward, meet individually with students to discuss their results. Use their responses to plan further instruction and review.

Model the Skill

◆ Hand out the Day 1 activity page.

◆ **Say:** *Words are made up of smaller parts called syllables. If we listen carefully to a word, we can hear the syllables, or parts, in the word.*

◆ Say the word **picnic**, stressing each syllable. Tell students that **picnic** is made up of two smaller parts, or syllables. Say **picnic** again and clap once for each syllable. Now have students say and clap **picnic** with you.

◆ Direct students' attention to the activity page. **Say:** *We're going on a picnic. First, we'll pack things with one syllable. Can we pack grapes?* Say and clap the word **grapes** with students. Explain that **grapes** has one syllable. Ask them to color in the grapes. Repeat with **nuts.**

◆ **Say:** *Now we will pack things with two syllables. Can we pack a sandwich?* Say and clap the word **sandwich** with students. Explain that **sandwich** has two syllables. Then have them color the sandwich. Repeat with **carrot.**

◆ Then play "Zippity Dippity" (right) using students' names to help them practice segmenting words into syllables:

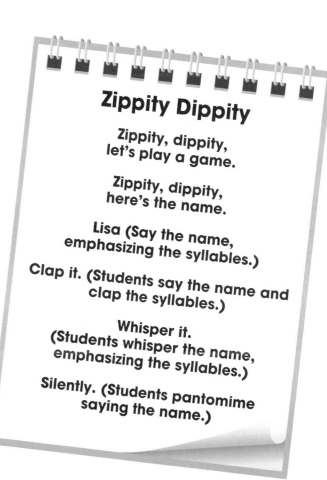

Zippity Dippity

Zippity, dippity,
let's play a game.

Zippity, dippity,
here's the name.

Lisa (Say the name,
emphasizing the syllables.)

Clap it. (Students say the name and
clap the syllables.)

Whisper it.
(Students whisper the name,
emphasizing the syllables.)

Silently. (Students pantomime
saying the name.)

Picnic Time!

Ask students to say each picture aloud and color the pictures that have two syllables.

Name _____

Syllable Count

**Ask students to say the name of each picture and clap the syllables.
Then ask them to color the pictures whose names have just one syllable.**

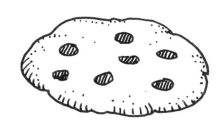

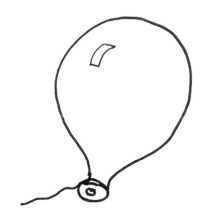

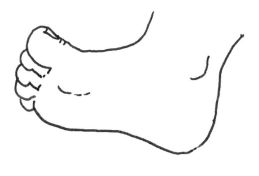

One or Two? Yellow or Blue?

Ask students to say the name of each picture and clap the syllables.
Tell them to draw a yellow circle around pictures with two syllables
and a blue circle around pictures with one syllable.

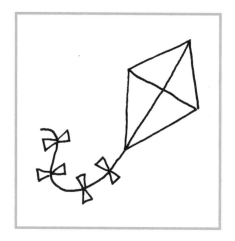

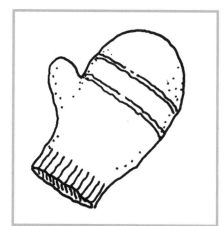

1, 2, 3

Ask students to cut out the picture cards. Ask them to name each one and to clap the syllables. Have them glue the picture under the 1, 2, or 3 to show how many syllables they hear.

1	2	3

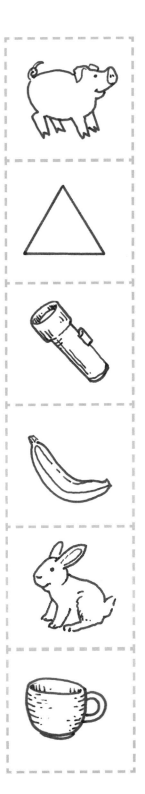

Assessment

Ask students to say the name of the pictures and clap the syllables.
Ask them to circle the 1 or the 2 to show how many syllables they hear.

1
2

1
2

1
2

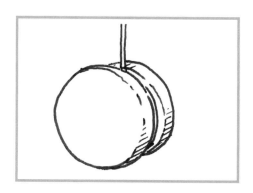
1
2

1
2

1
2

Ask students to listen as you say each word. Have them tally or write the number of syllables they hear.

1. _____

2. _____

Overview   Identifying Initial Sounds

Directions and Sample Answers for Activity Pages

Day 1	See "Model the Skill" below.
Day 2	Read aloud the title and directions. Have students name each picture. Then help students match pictures that begin with the same sound. (**fan/fork; baby/box; lion/log; cake/cat; ring/rake**)
Day 3	Read aloud the title and directions. Have students cut out the pictures and name them. Help them sort the pictures by the sound they begin with, **/b/** as in **box** or **/n/** as in **net**. (**Box: ball, bus, bat**; **Net: necklace, nail, nut**)
Day 4	Read aloud the title and directions. Invite students to name each picture. Then help students circle the pictures that start with **/m/** and draw a square around pictures that start with **/d/**. (**/m/: mouse, moon, mittens, man; /d/: dog, doll, door, duck**)
Day 5	Read aloud the directions and name the pictures together. Allow time for students to draw pictures that begin with the same sounds as the pictures on the page. Afterward, meet individually with students to discuss their results. Use their responses to plan further instruction and review.

Model the Skill

◆ Point to a book and **say:** *The first sound in* **book** *is* **/b/**. Be sure to emphasize both the **/b/** in the word and the **/b/** in isolation.

◆ Point to other items in the classroom that have a single beginning consonant sound, such as **desk, light, map, teacher,** and **door**. Help students identify the beginning sounds as you or they say the item's name aloud.

◆ Hand out the Day 1 activity page.

◆ Sing these words to the tune of "London Bridges Is Falling Down":
What's the first sound that you hear,
that you hear,
that you hear?
What's the first sound that you hear in
fish, fish, fish?

◆ **Say:** *That's right!* **Fish** *begins with the* **/f/** *sound. Now color in the fish.*

◆ Repeat this song with the other pictures on the activity page: **/b/: boat, /m/: man, /s/: sun.**

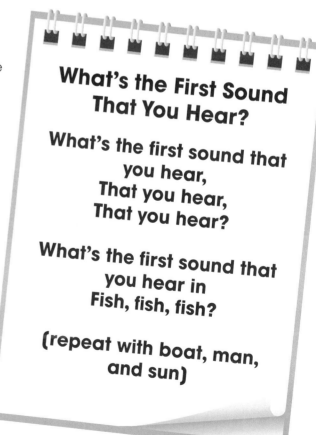

What's the First Sound That You Hear?

What's the first sound that you hear,
That you hear,
That you hear?

What's the first sound that you hear in
Fish, fish, fish?

(repeat with boat, man, and sun)

What's the First Sound That You Hear?

Sing the song to students for each initial sound and have them color in the pictures.

Sound Match

Ask students to name each picture in the left-hand column, then draw a line to the picture in the right-hand column whose name begins with the same sound.

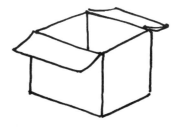

Box or Net?

Ask students to cut out the pictures and say the name of each one. Ask them to glue pictures that start with the same sound as *box* in the box and the pictures that start with the same sound as *net* in the net.

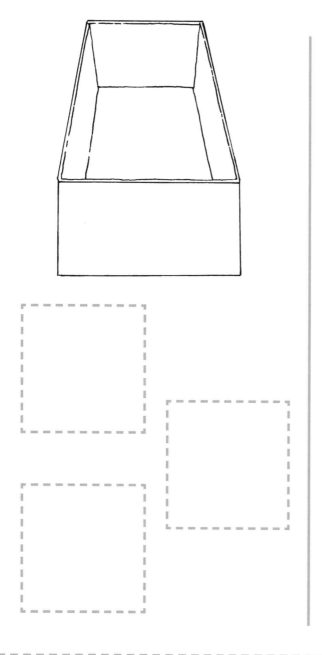

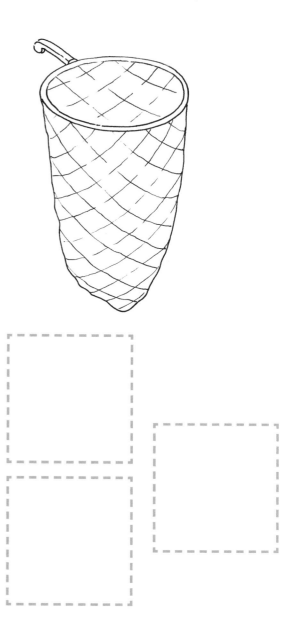

Letter Sounds

Ask students to say the name of each picture.
Circle the pictures that start with /m/ as in *mom*.
Draw a square around pictures that begin with /d/ as in *dad*.

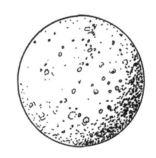

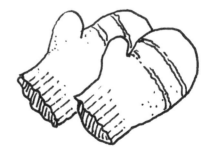

Assessment

Ask students to say the name of each picture. Have them draw a picture of something else that begins with the same sound in the box.

Overview Segmenting Compound Words

Directions and Sample Answers for Activity Pages

Day 1	See "Model the Skill" below.
Day 2	Read aloud the title and directions. Help students name each picture. Then help students match pictures to create a compound word. (**rainbow; football; teacup; firefly**)
Day 3	Read aloud the title and directions. Help students cut out picture cards and name them. Then help them put the picture cards together to form the compound words pictured at the end of each equation. (**wheel** + **chair** = **wheelchair; finger** + **nail** = **fingernail; cup** + **cake** = **cupcake**)
Day 4	Pair students to play the game. Help students cut out and shuffle the picture cards, then lay the cards facedown. Players take turns turning over two cards. If the cards make a compound word, the player says the word and keeps the cards. If the cards do not make a compound word, the player turns them back over and it's the second player's turn. (**pancake; firefly; wallpaper; rainbow; bullfrog; drumstick; haircut; jellyfish**)
Day 5	Read aloud the directions and name the pictures together. Allow time for students to identify which pictures form a compound word with **ball**. Afterward, meet individually with students to discuss their results. Use their responses to plan further instruction and review.

Model the Skill

◆ Point to a notebook and **say:** *The word **notebook** is made up of two words, **note** and **book**. When two words join together to form a new word, such as **notebook**, it is a compound word.*

◆ **Say:** *I am going to take away the first part of **notebook**. Tell me the second part of the word. That's right, **notebook** without **note** is just **book**.*

◆ Hand out the Day 1 activity page. **Say:** *Let's go on a compound word hunt. When you find a picture of a compound word, color it in. Is **armchair** a compound word?* Have students confirm by saying the word and pausing between the two parts: **arm** (pause) **chair**. Allow time for students to color the armchair.

◆ **Say:** *Is **lampshade** a compound word? I am going to take away the first part, **lamp**, away. Is **shade** a word? Yes! Is **lamp** a word? Yes! So **lampshade** is a compound word.* Ask students to color it in. Repeat with **earring, doorknob,** and **nightlight.**

◆ Invite students to share other compound words they know.

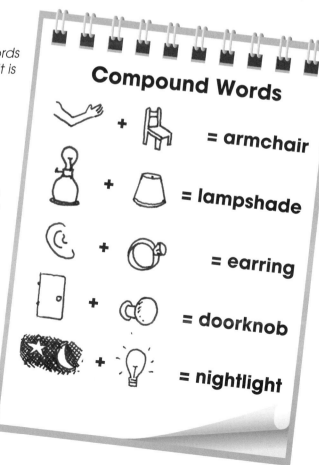

Compound Words

+ = armchair

+ = lampshade

+ = earring

+ = doorknob

+ = nightlight

Compound Word Search

Ask students to color in the pictures of the compound words.

Match Up

Ask students to say the name of the pictures in both columns. Then help them create compound words by matching pictures in the left column with pictures in the right column.

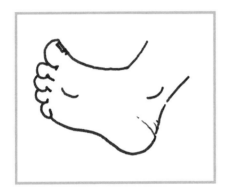

Make a Word

Ask students to cut out the picture cards. Help them put together the two cards whose names form one of the compound words pictured. Then tell them to glue the cards in place.

Name _____

Compound-Word Concentration

Ask student pairs to cut out the pictures and use them to play a compound word-making game of Concentration.

Assessment

Ask students to say the name of each picture, including the one in the middle. Have them draw a line from the ball to each picture that makes a compound word with *ball*.

Overview Aa, Bb

Directions and Sample Answers for Activity Pages

Day 1	See "Model the Letter A" below. Ask students to raise their hands if their first or last name begins with the letter **A**. Invite those students to write their names on chart paper. Circle the letter **A** in each name. Tell students this is the letter **A**. After, hand out the Day 1 activity page, read aloud the title and directions for the students.
Day 2	See "Model the Letter a" below. Then invite students to look for the letter **a** around the classroom—on books, posters, labels, etc. Have them share their findings with the class. After, hand out and read aloud the title and directions for the activity page.
Day 3	See "Model the Letter B" below. Then ask students to raise their hands if their first or last name begins with the letter **B**. Invite those students to write their names on chart paper. Circle the letter **B** in each name. Tell students this is the letter **B**. After, hand out the Day 3 activity poge, read aloud the title and directions for the students.
Day 4	See "Model the Letter b" below. Then invite students to look for the letter **b** inside books, magazines, and other materials. Check their findings to make sure they are correct. After, read aloud the title and directions for the activity.
Day 5	Read aloud the directions. Allow time for students to complete the task. Afterward, meet individually with students to discuss their results. Use their responses to plan further instruction and review.

Model the Letter A

◆ Write the letter **A** on the chalkboard. Tell students this is uppercase **A**. Trace your finger over the letter **A** starting at the top, and **say:** *A is slant left and down, lift, slant right and down, lift, cross in the middle.*

Model the Letter a

◆ Write the letter **a** on the chalkboard. Tell students this is lowercase **a**. Trace your finger over the letter **a** starting at the top, and **say:** *a is circle back all the way around, push up, pull down.*

Model the Letter B

◆ Write the letter **B** on the chalkboard. Tell students this is uppercase **B**. Trace your finger over the letter **B** starting at the top, and **say:** *B is pull down, push up to the top, around and around.*

Model the Letter b

◆ Write the letter **b** on the chalkboard. Tell students this is lowercase **b**. Trace your finger over the letter **b** starting at the top, and **say:** *b is pull down, push up to the middle and around.*

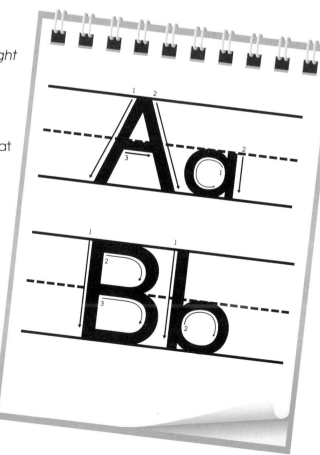

A Is for Apple

Ask students to find all the apples with the letter *A* and color them red.
Ask students to color the rest of the apples yellow.

Trace and write.

Unit 6 • *Everyday Phonics Intervention Activities Grade K* • ©2010 Newmark Learning, LLC

Tic-Tac-Toe

Ask student pairs to cut out the letters. Then ask them to take turns putting their letters on the tic-tac-toe board. The first to get three in a row wins!

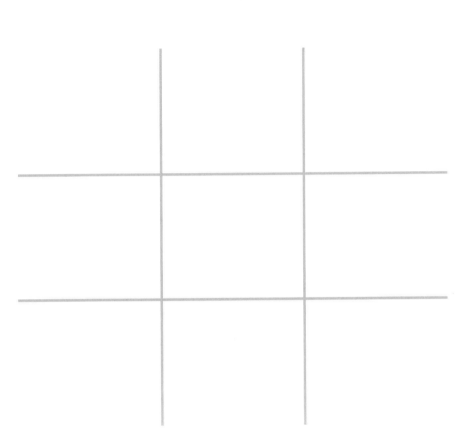

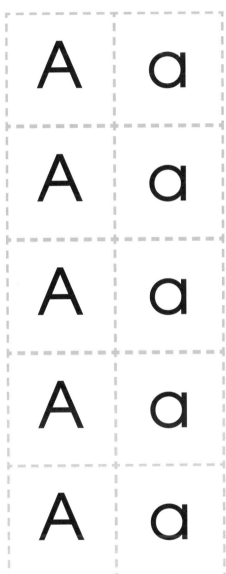

Trace and write.

Mystery Letter

Ask students to color the letter _B_ spaces.

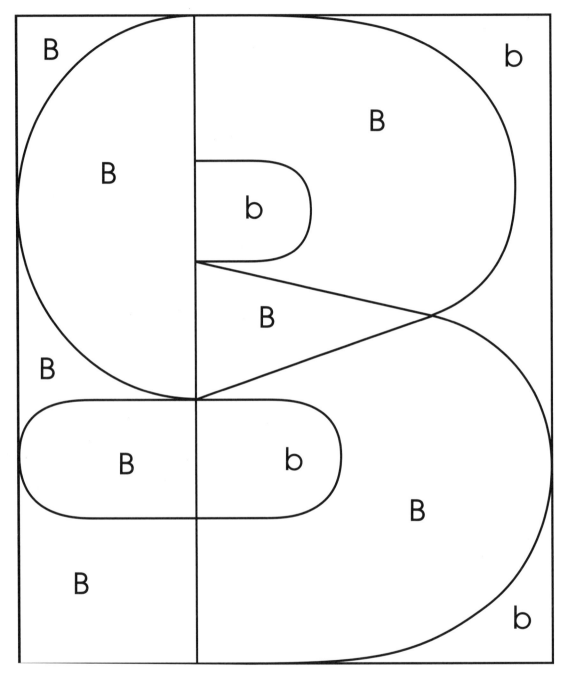

Trace and write.

Balloons

**Ask students to color the balloons that have the letter *b* blue
and the balloons that have the letter *B* brown.**

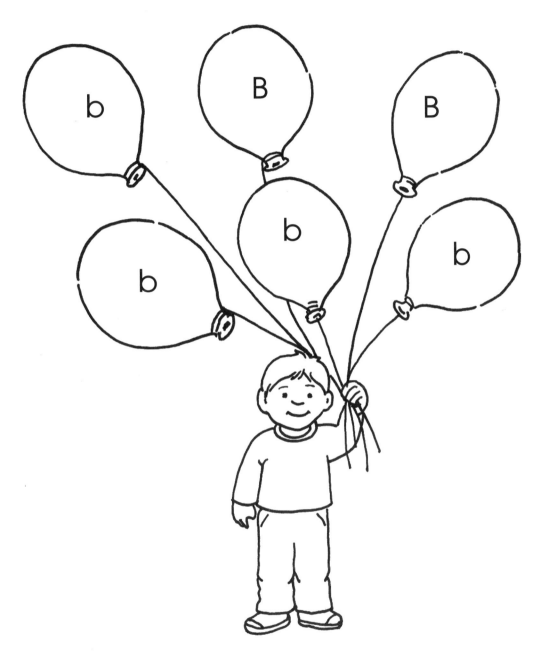

Trace and write.

Name _____

Assessment

Ask students to draw lines connecting the matching letters in each picture.

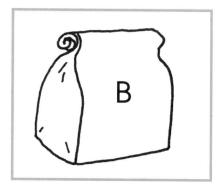

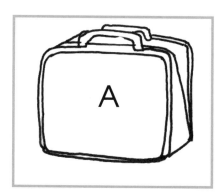

Overview Cc, Dd

Directions and Sample Answers for Activity Pages

Day 1	See "Model the Letter C" below. Ask students to raise their hands if their first or last name begins with the letter **C**. Then invite those students to write their names on chart paper. Circle the letter **C** in each name. Tell students this is the letter **C**. After, hand out the Day 1 activity page and read aloud the title and directions for the students.
Day 2	See "Model the Letter c" below. Then invite students to look for the letter **c** around the classroom—on books, posters, labels, etc. Ask them to share their findings with the class. After, hand out the Day 2 activity page and read aloud the title and directions for the students.
Day 3	See "Model the Letter D" below. Then ask students to raise their hands if their first or last name begins with the letter **D**. Invite those students to write their names on chart paper. Circle the letter **D** in each name. Tell students this is the letter **D**. After, hand out the Day 3 activity page and read aloud the title and directions for the students.
Day 4	See "Model the Letter d" below. Then invite students to look for the letter **d** inside books, magazines, and other materials. Check their findings to make sure they are correct. After, hand out the Day 4 activity page and read aloud the title and directions for the students.
Day 5	Read aloud the directions. Allow time for students to complete the task. Afterward, meet individually with students to discuss their results. Use their responses to plan further instruction and review.

Model the Letter C

◆ Write the letter **C** on the chalkboard. Tell students this is uppercase **C**. Trace your finger over the letter **C** starting at the top, and **say:** *C is circle back and open.*

Model the Letter c

◆ Write the letter **c** on the chalkboard. Tell students this is lowercase **c**. Trace your finger over the letter **c** starting at the top, and **say:** *c is circle back and open.*

Model the Letter D

◆ Write the letter **D** on the chalkboard. Tell students this is uppercase **D**. Trace your finger over the letter **D**, starting at the top and **say:** *D is pull down, lift, curve forward.*

Model the Letter d

◆ Write the letter **d** on the chalkboard. Tell students this is lowercase **d**. Trace your finger over the letter **d**, starting at the top and **say:** *d is circle back around, push to the top, pull down.*

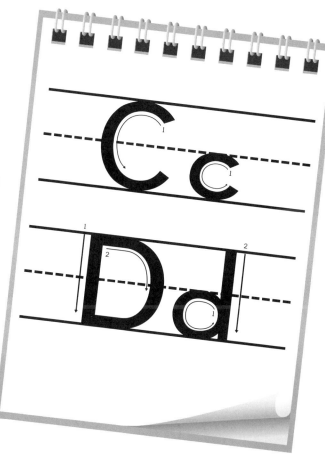

Cat's Car

Ask students to help get Cat home by connecting all the *C* letters.

C	B	A	b	a
C	A	C	C	b
A	C	a	C	B
B	b	A	a	C

Trace and write.

Cookie Time

Ask students to cut out the cookies at the bottom. Ask them to glue the cookies with the letter *c* in the cookie jar. Then glue the cookies with the letter *C* on the cookie sheet.

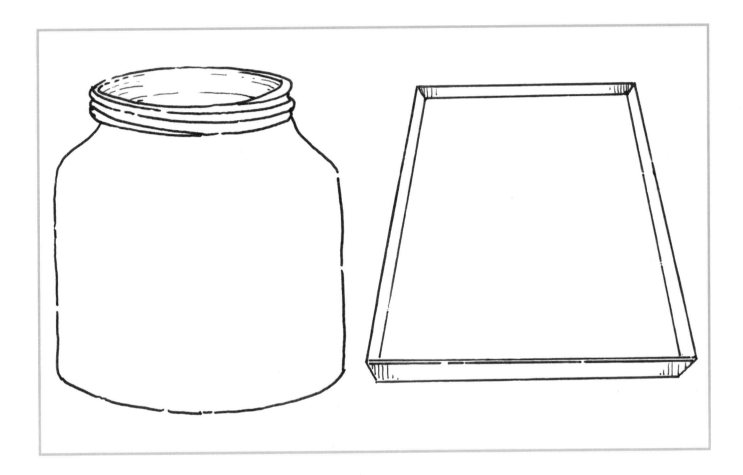

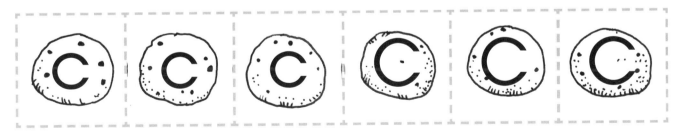

Trace and write.

Mystery Letter

Ask students to color the letter *D* spaces.

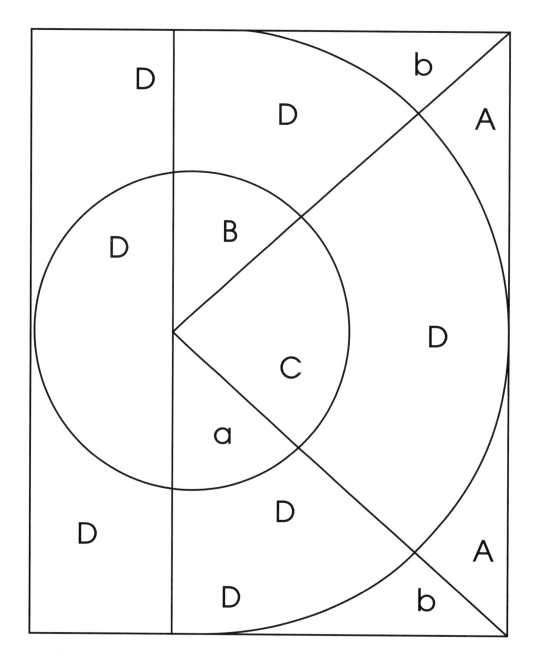

Trace and write.

Unit 7 • Everyday Phonics Intervention Activities Grade K • ©2010 Newmark Learning, LLC

Dog Days

Ask students to color the dogs that have the letter *d* brown.
Then ask them to color the dogs that have the letter *D* black.

Trace and write.

Name _____

Assessment

Ask students to name the letters in each row. Then ask them to circle the letters that match the first letter in each row.

c	c b c a c
D	d D D B A
C	D a C C B
d	d b b D d

Overview Ee, Ff

Directions and Sample Answers for Activity Pages

Day 1	See "Model the Letter E" below. Ask students to raise their hands if their first or last name begins with the letter **E**. Invite those students to write their names on chart paper. Circle the letter **E** in each name. Tell students this is the letter **E**. After, hand out the Day 1 activity page and read aloud the title and directions for the students.
Day 2	See "Model the Letter e" below. Then Invite students to look for the letter **e** around the classroom—on books, posters, labels, etc. Have them share their findings with the class. After, hand out the Day 2 activity page and read aloud the title and directions.
Day 3	See "Model the Letter F" below. Then ask students to raise their hands if their first or last name begins with the letter **F**. Invite those students to write their names on chart paper. Circle the letter **F** in each name. Tell students this is the letter **F**. After, hand out the Day 3 activity page and read aloud the title and directions for the students.
Day 4	See "Model the Letter f" below. Then Invite students to look for the letter **f** inside books, magazines, and other materials. Check their findings to make sure they are correct. After, hand out the Day 4 activity page and read aloud the title and directions.
Day 5	Read aloud the directions. Allow time for students to complete the task. Afterward, meet individually with students to discuss their results. Use their responses to plan further instruction and review.

Model the Letter E

◆ Write the letter **E** on the chalkboard. Tell students this is uppercase **E**. Trace your finger over the letter **E**, starting at the top, and **say:** *E is pull down, lift, on the top slide right, in the middle slide right, on the bottom slide right.*

Model the Letter e

◆ Write the letter **e** on the chalkboard. Tell students this is lowercase **e**. Trace your finger over the letter **e** and **say:** *e is slide right, circle left.*

Model the Letter F

◆ Write the letter **F** on the chalkboard. Tell students this is uppercase **F**. Trace your finger over the letter **F**, starting at the top and **say:** *F is pull down, lift, on the top slide right, in the middle slide right.*

Model the Letter f

◆ Write the letter **f** on the chalkboard. Tell students this is lowercase **f**. Trace your finger over the letter **f**, starting at the top and **say:** *f is curve back from the top, cross in the middle.*

Name _____

Build an E

Ask students to color the pieces. Then ask them to cut them out and glue them on to the paper to build an *E*.

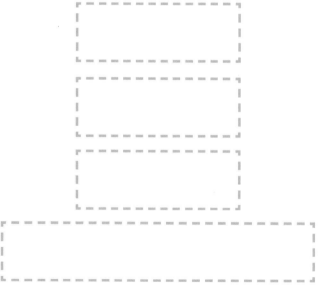

Trace and write.

Egg Hunt

Ask students to color the eggs with the letter *E* blue and the eggs with the letter *e* yellow.

Trace and write.

Mystery Picture

What do spring showers bring? To find out, ask students to color the letter *F* spaces yellow, the uppercase letter *E* spaces green, and the lowercase letter *e* spaces blue.

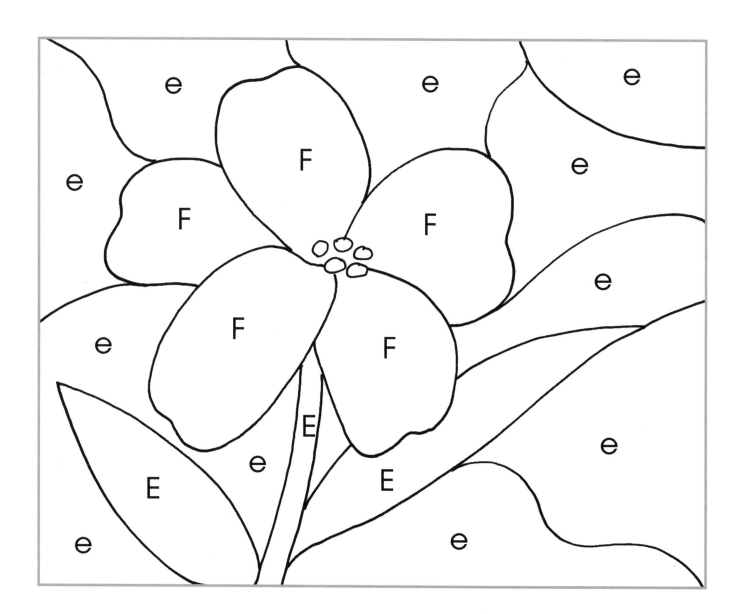

Trace and write.

Leap Frog

Ask students to help Frog across the lake by connecting lilypads with the letter *f*.

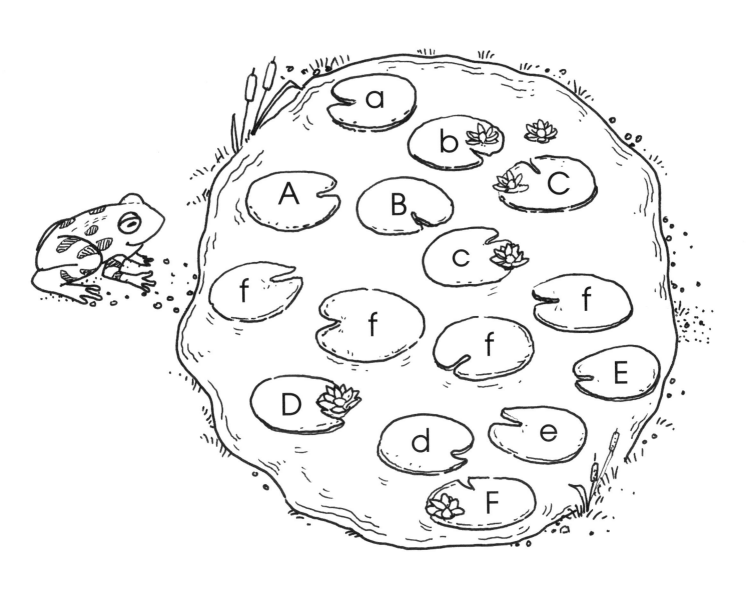

Trace and write.

Name _____

Assessment

Ask students to draw lines to match the letters on the fish to the letters on the fishbowls.

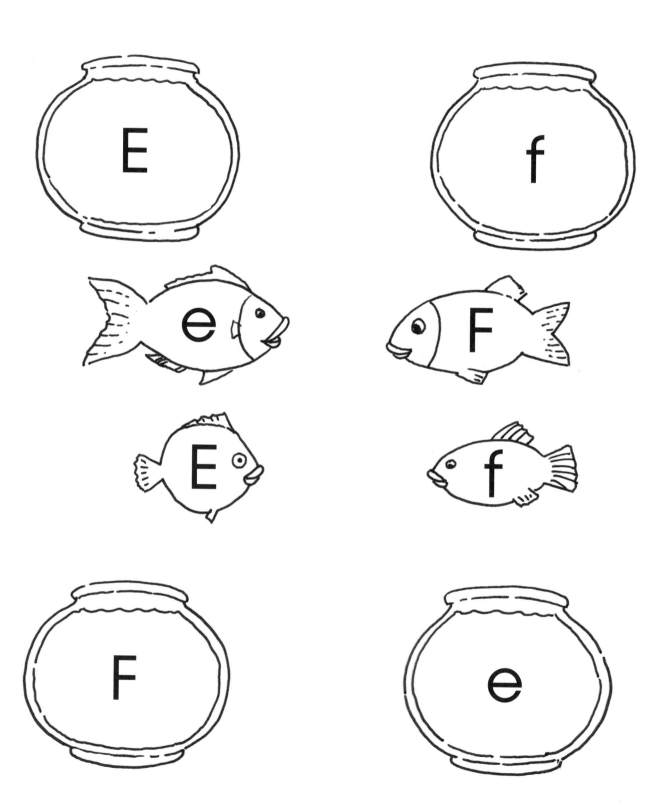

Overview Gg, Hh

Directions and Sample Answers for Activity Pages

Day 1	See "Model the Letter G" below. Ask students to raise their hands if their first or last name begins with the letter **G**. Invite those students to write their names on chart paper. Circle the letter **G** in each name. Tell students this is the letter **G**. After, hand out the Day 1 activity page and read aloud the title and directions for the students.
Day 2	See "Model the Letter g" below. Then invite students to look for the letter **g** around the classroom—on books, posters, labels, etc. Have them share their findings with the class. After, hand out the Day 2 activity page and read aloud the title and directions.
Day 3	See "Model the Letter H" below. Ask students to raise their hands if their first or last name begins with the letter **H**. Invite those students to write their names on chart paper. Circle the letter **H** in each name. Tell students this is the letter **H**. After, hand out the Day 3 activity page and read aloud the title and directions for the students.
Day 4	See "Model the Letter h" below. Then invite students to look for the letter **h** inside books, magazines, and other materials. Check their findings to make sure they are correct. After, hand out the Day 4 activity page and read aloud the title and directions.
Day 5	Read aloud the directions. Allow time for students to complete the task. Afterward, meet individually with students to discuss their results. Use their responses to plan further instruction and review.

Model the Letter G

◆ Write the letter **G** on the chalkboard. Tell students this is uppercase **G**. Trace your finger over the letter **G**, starting at the top, and **say:** *G is circle back at the top, slide left in the middle.*

Model the Letter g

◆ Write the letter g on the chalkboard. Tell students this is lowercase **g**. Trace your finger over the letter **g**, starting at the top, and **say:** *g is circle back around, push up, pull down, curve in.*

Model the Letter H

◆ Write the letter **H** on the chalkboard. Tell students this is uppercase **H**. Trace your finger over the letter **H**, starting at the top and **say:** *H is pull down, lift, pull down, cross in the middle.*

Model the Letter h

◆ Write the letter **h** on the chalkboard. Tell students this is lowercase **h**. Trace your finger over the letter **h**, starting at the top and **say:** *h is pull down, push up to the middle, curve forward, pull down.*

G in the Box

Ask students to write the letter _G_ in each box.

Trace and write.

Tic-Tac-Toe

Ask student pairs to cut out the letters. Then have them take turns putting their letters on the tic-tac-toe board. The first to get three in a row wins!

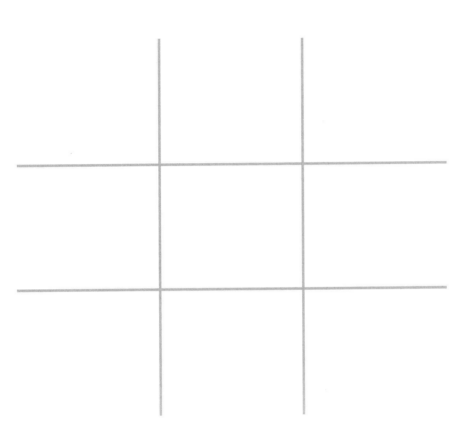

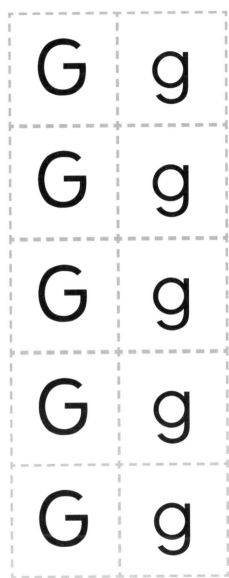

Trace and write.

Name _____

Mystery Picture

Ask students to color the *H* spaces brown, and the *A* spaces yellow to reveal a mystery picture.

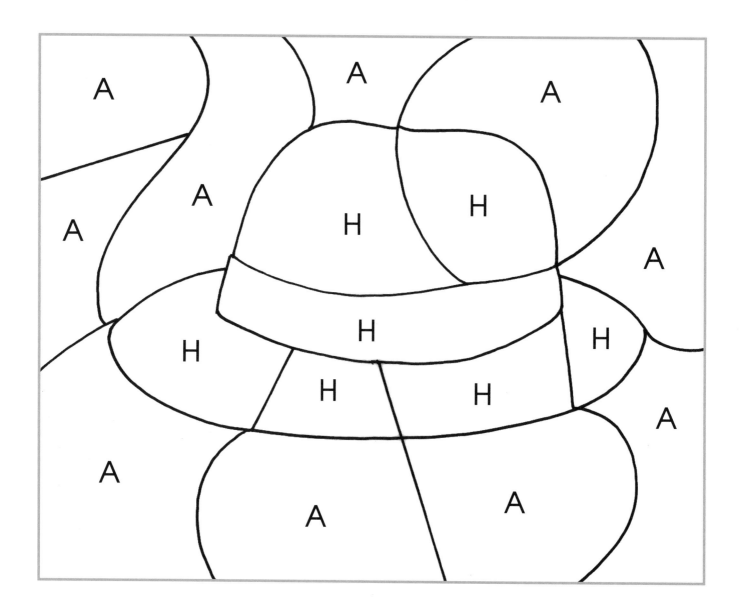

Trace and write.

Unit 9 • Everyday Phonics Intervention Activities Grade K • ©2010 Newmark Learning, LLC

Name _____

Hare Hops Home

**Ask student pairs to help Hare hop home. First connect all the *h* letters.
Then color Hare and her home.**

h	h	A	h	E
f	D	h	F	h
A	C	G	c	h
c	b	g	a	h

Trace and write.

Name _____

Assessment

Ask students to draw lines connecting the matching letters in each picture.

G

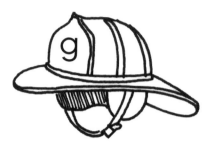 g

h

 G

g

 H

H

 h

Overview Ii, Jj

Directions and Sample Answers for Activity Pages

Day 1	See "Model the Letter I" below. Then ask students to raise their hands if their first or last name begins with the letter **I**. Invite those students to write their names on chart paper. Circle the letter **I** in each name. After, hand out the Day 1 activity page and read aloud the title and directions for the students.
Day 2	See "Model the Letter i" below. Then invite students to look for the letter **i** around the classroom—on books, posters, labels, etc. Have them share their findings with the class. After, hand out the Day 2 activity page and read aloud the title and directions for the students.
Day 3	See "Model the Letter J" below. Ask students to raise their hands if their first or last name begins with the letter **J**. Invite those students to write their names on chart paper. Circle the letter **J** in each name. Tell students this is the letter **J**. After, hand out the Day 3 activity page and read aloud the title and directions for the students.
Day 4	See "Model the Letter j" below. Invite students to look for the letter **j** inside books, magazines, and other materials. Check their findings to make sure they are correct. After, hand out the Day 4 activity page and read aloud the title and directions for the students.
Day 5	Read aloud the directions. Allow time for students to complete the task. Afterward, meet individually with students to discuss their results. Use their responses to plan further instruction and review.

Model the Letter I

◆ Write the letter **I** on the chalkboard. Tell students this is uppercase **I**. Trace your finger over the letter **I**, starting at the top, and **say:** *I is pull down, across at the top, across at the bottom.*

Model the Letter i

◆ Write the letter **i** on the chalkboard. Tell students this is lowercase **i**. Trace your finger over the letter **i**, starting at the top, and **say:** *i is pull down, dot at the top.*

Model the Letter J

◆ Write the letter **J** on the chalkboard. Tell students this is uppercase **J**. Trace your finger over the letter **J**, starting at the top, and **say:** *J is pull down, curve back, across at the top.*

Model the Letter j

◆ Write the letter **j** on the chalkboard. Tell students this is lowercase **j**. Trace your finger over the letter **j**, starting at the top, and **say:** *j is pull down, curve back, dot at the top.*

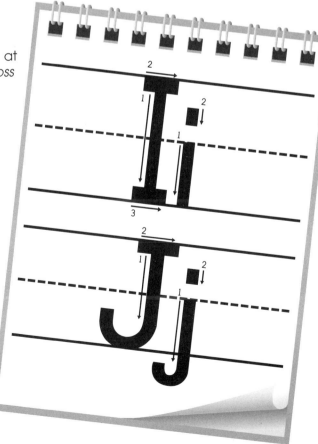

Build an I

Ask students to color the pieces. Then help students cut and glue each piece onto the paper to create an _I_.

Trace and write.

We All Scream for Ice Cream

Ask students to color the scoops that have the letter *i* green. Ask students to color the scoops that have the letter *I* pink and to color the cone brown.

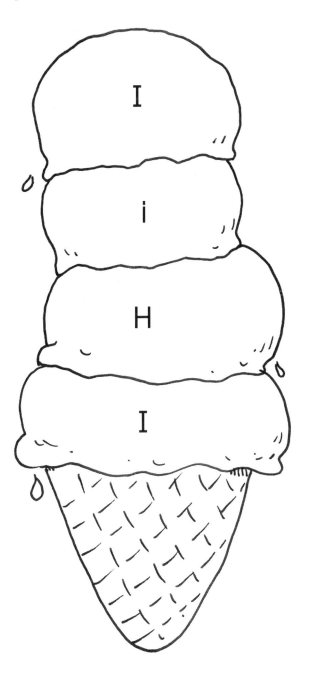

Trace and write.

Mystery Letter

Ask students to color the letter *J* spaces blue and all the other letter spaces red.

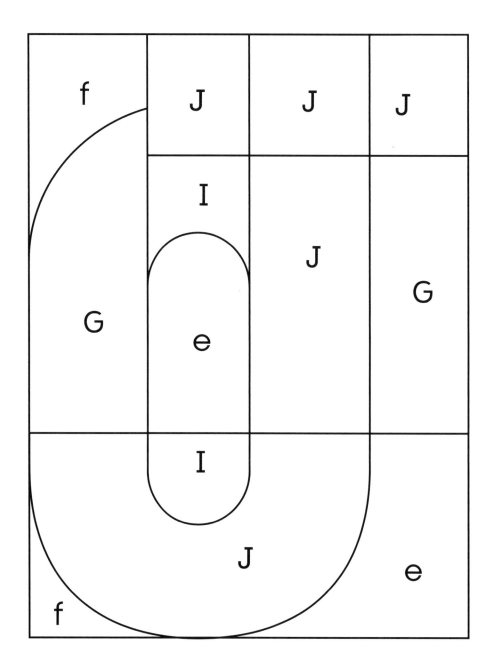

Trace and write.

Unit 10 • Everyday Phonics Intervention Activities Grade K • ©2010 Newmark Learning, LLC

Jack and Jill

Ask students to help Jack up the hill to Jill by connecting stepping stones with the letter *j*.

Trace and write.

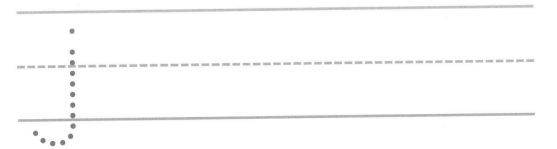

Name _____

Assessment

Ask students to name the letters in each row. Then ask them to circle the letters that match the first letter in each row.

J	J	j	I	J	I
I	J	J	I	i	I
i	j	i	i	j	J
j	j	i	J	i	j

Unit 10 • Everyday Phonics Intervention Activities Grade K • ©2010 Newmark Learning, LLC

Overview Kk, Ll

Directions and Sample Answers for Activity Pages

Day 1	See "Model the Letter K" below. Then ask students to raise their hands if their first or last name begins with the letter **K**. Invite those students to write their names on chart paper. Circle the letter **K** in each name. Tell students this is the letter **K**. After, hand out the Day 1 activity page and read aloud the title and directions for the students.
Day 2	See "Model the Letter k" below. Then invite students to look for the letter **k** around the classroom—on books, posters, labels, etc. Have them share their findings with the class. After, hand out the Day 2 activity page and read aloud the title and directions for the students.
Day 3	See "Model the Letter L" below. Then ask students to raise their hands if their first or last name begins with the letter **L**. Invite those students to write their names on chart paper. Circle the letter **L** in each name. After, hand out the Day 3 activity page and read aloud the title and directions for the students.
Day 4	See "Model the Letter l" below. Then invite students to look for the letter **l** inside books, magazines, and other materials. Check their findings to make sure they are correct. After, hand out the Day 4 activity page and read aloud the title and directions for the students.
Day 5	Read aloud the directions. Allow time for students to complete the task. Afterward, meet individually with students to discuss their results. Use their responses to plan further instruction and review.

Model the Letter K

◆ Write the letter **K** on the chalkboard. Tell students this is uppercase **K**. Trace your finger over the letter **K**, starting at the top, and **say: K** *is pull down, slant in, slant out.*

Model the Letter k

◆ Write the letter **k** on the chalkboard. Tell students this is lowercase **k**. Trace your finger over the letter **k**, starting at the top, and **say: k** *is pull down, slant in, slant out.*

Model the Letter L

◆ Write the letter **L** on the chalkboard. Tell students this is uppercase **L**. Trace your finger over the letter **L**, starting at the top, and **say: L** *is pull down, slide right.*

Model the Letter l

◆ Write the letter **l** on the chalkboard. Tell students this is lowercase **l**. Trace your finger over the letter **l**, starting at the top, and **say: l** *is pull down.*

King's Maze

Ask students to help the king through the maze. First connect all the *K* letters. Then color the king and his castle.

K   E   B   A   C

K   B   K   K   H

G   K   H   F   K

C   E   I   B   K

Trace and write.

Tic-Tac-Toe

Ask student pairs to cut out the letters. Then ask them to take turns putting their letters on the tic-tac-toe board. The first to get three in a row wins!

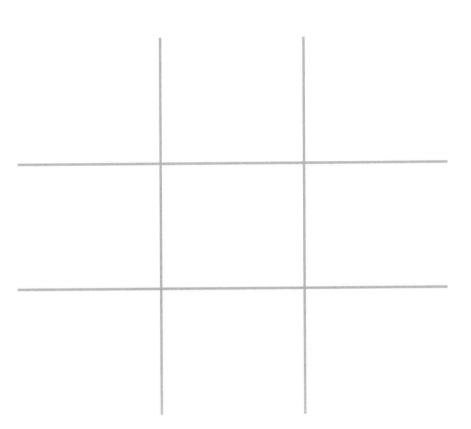

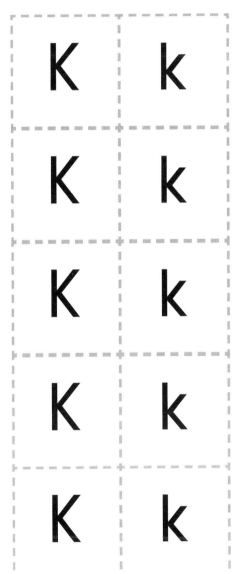

Trace and write.

Mystery Letter

Ask students to color each box with the letter *L* to see the mystery letter.

L	K	I	E
L	C	J	A
L	F	I	H
L	L	L	I

Trace and write.

Name _____

Lilly's Lollipops

Color the lollipops with the letter *l* orange. Color the lollipops with the letter *L* yellow.

Trace and write.

Assessment

Ask students to draw a string from the letters on the kids' shirts to the matching kites.

Unit 11 • *Everyday Phonics Intervention Activities Grade K* • ©2010 Newmark Learning, LLC

Overview Mm, Nn

Directions and Sample Answers for Activity Pages

Day 1	See "Model the Letter M" below. Then ask students to raise their hands if their first or last name begins with the letter **M**. Invite those students to write their names on chart paper. Circle the letter **M** in each name. Tell students this is the letter **M**. After, hand out the Day 1 activity page and read aloud the title and directions for the students.
Day 2	See "Model the Letter m" below. Then invite students to look for the letter **m** around the classroom—on books, posters, labels, etc. Have them share their findings with the class. After, hand out the Day 2 activity page and read aloud the title and directions for the students.
Day 3	See "Model the Letter N" below. Then ask students to raise their hands if their first or last name begins with the letter **N**. Invite those students to write their names on chart paper. Circle the letter **N** in each name. Tell students this is the letter **N**. After, hand out the Day 3 activity page and read aloud the title and directions for the students.
Day 4	See "Model the Letter n" below. Then invite students to look for the letter **n** inside books, magazines, and other materials. Check their findings to make sure they are correct. After, hand out the Day 4 activity page and read aloud the title and directions for the students.
Day 5	Read aloud the directions. Allow time for students to complete the task. Afterward, meet individually with students to discuss their results. Use their responses to plan further instruction and review.

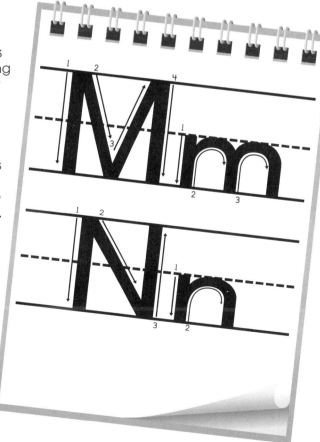

Model the Letter M

◆ Write the letter **M** on the chalkboard. Tell students this is uppercase **M**. Trace your finger over the letter **M**, starting at the top, and **say:** *M is pull down, lift, slant right, slant up, pull down.*

Model the Letter m

◆ Write the letter **m** on the chalkboard. Tell students this is lowercase **m**. Trace your finger over the letter **m**, starting at the top, and **say:** *m is pull down, push up, curve forward, pull down, push up, curve forward, pull down.*

Model the Letter N

◆ Write the letter **N** on the chalkboard. Tell students this is uppercase **N**. Trace your finger over the letter **N**, starting at the top, and **say:** *N is pull down, lift, slant right, push up.*

Model the Letter n

◆ Write the letter **n** on the chalkboard. Tell students this is lowercase **n**. Trace your finger over the letter **n**, starting at the top, and **say:** *n is pull down, push up, curve forward, pull down.*

Name _____

Mouse Maze

Ask students to lead the mouse to his mom by coloring the letter *M* along the path.

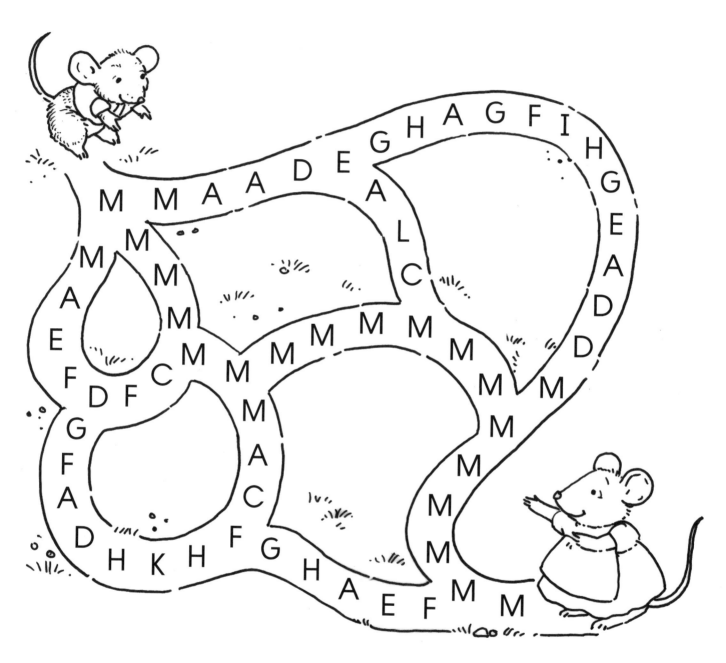

Trace and write.

Mixed-Up Marbles

Ask students to cut out the marbles at the bottom of the page. Help them glue the marbles with the letter *m* in the jar labeled *m*. Then help them glue the marbles with the letter *M* in the jar labeled *M*.

Trace and write.

Mystery Letter

Ask students to color each box with the letter **N** to see the mystery letter.

N	m	m	m	N
N	N	L	m	N
N	m	N	M	N
N	m	L	N	N
N	M	m	m	N

Trace and write.

Unit 12 • *Everyday Phonics Intervention Activities Grade K* • ©2010 Newmark Learning, LLC

Chock Full of Nuts

Ask students to color the nuts with the letter *n* brown and the nuts with the letter *N* purple.

Trace and write.

Assessment

Ask students to name the letters in each row. Then ask them to circle the letters that match the first letter in each row.

N	M N N m n
n	n m m n N
M	N M M n n
m	m n m m n

Overview   Oo, Pp

Directions and Sample Answers for Activity Pages

Day 1	See "Model the Letter O" below. Then ask students to raise their hands if their first or last name begins with the letter **O**. Invite those students to write their names on chart paper. Circle the letter **O** in each name. Tell students this is the letter **O**. After, hand out the Day 1 activity page and read aloud the title and directions for the students.
Day 2	See "Model the Letter o" below. Then invite students to look for the letter **o** around the classroom—on books, posters, labels, etc. Have them share their findings with the class. After, hand out the Day 2 activity page and read aloud the title and directions for the students.
Day 3	See "Model the Letter P" below. Then ask students to raise their hands if their first or last name begins with the letter **P**. Invite those students to write their names on chart paper. Circle the letter **P** in each name. Tell students this is the letter **P.** After, hand out the Day 3 activity page and read aloud the title and directions for the students.
Day 4	See "Model the Letter p" below. Then invite students to look for the letter **p** inside books, magazines, and other materials. Check their findings to make sure they are correct. After, hand out the Day 4 activity page and read aloud the title and directions for the students.
Day 5	Read aloud the directions. Allow time for students to complete the task. Afterward, meet individually with students to discuss their results. Use their responses to plan further instruction and review.

Model the Letter O

◆ Write the letter **O** on the chalkboard. Tell students this is uppercase **O**. Trace your finger over the letter **O**, starting at the top, and **say:** *O is circle around.*

Model the Letter o

◆ Write the letter **o** on the chalkboard. Tell students this is lowercase **o**. Trace your finger over the letter **o**, starting at the top, and **say:** *o is circle around.*

Model the Letter P

◆ Write the letter **P** on the chalkboard. Tell students this is uppercase **P**. Trace your finger over the letter **P**, starting at the top, and **say:** *P is pull down, push up, circle forward.*

Model the Letter p

◆ Write the letter **p** on the chalkboard. Tell students this is lowercase **p**. Trace your finger over the letter **p**, starting at the top, and **say:** *p is pull down, push up, circle forward.*

Oodles of Noodles

Ask students to circle each letter O in this oodles of noodles soup.

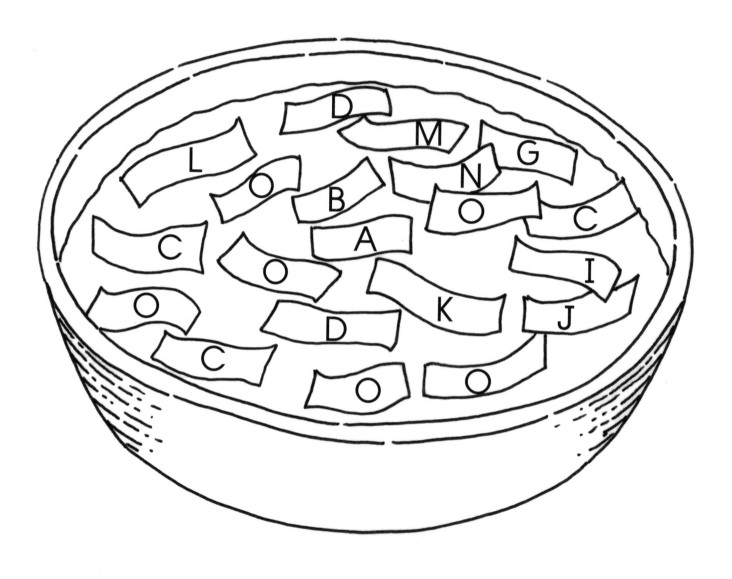

Trace and write.

Name _____

Tic-Tac-Toe

Ask student pairs to cut out the letters, taking care to keep the uppercase and lowercase letters separate. Then ask them to take turns putting their letters on the tic-tac-toe board. The first to get three in a row wins!

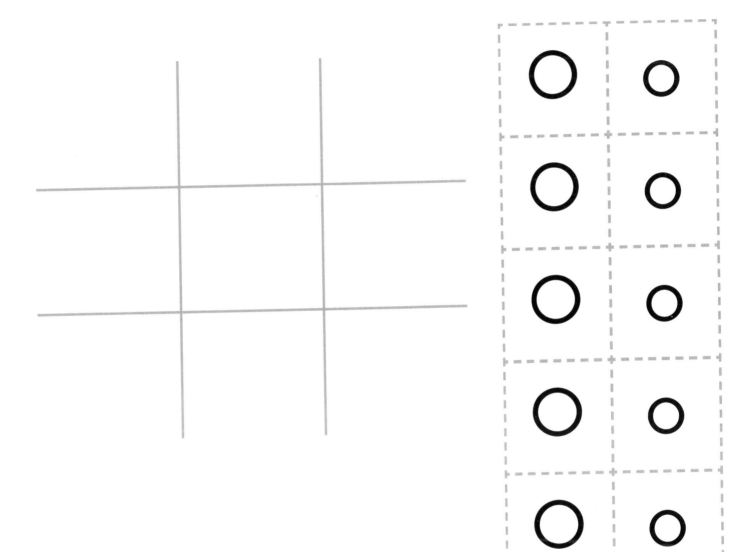

Trace and write.

Name _____

Pam's Pickles

Ask students to help Pam find her pickles by coloring each pickle with the letter *P*.

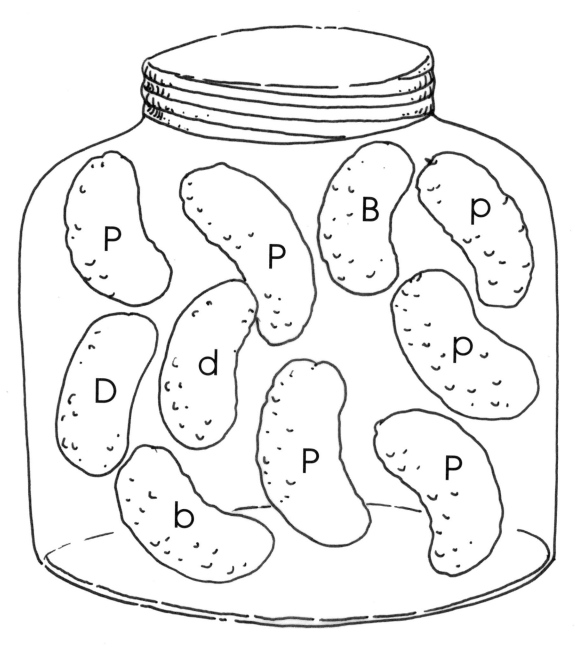

Trace and write.

Unit 13 • Everyday Phonics Intervention Activities Grade K • ©2010 Newmark Learning, LLC

Presents, Presents Everywhere

Ask students to color the presents with the letter *p* purple
and to color the presents with the letter *P* pink.

Trace and write.

Assessment

Ask students to draw lines to match the letters on the pumpkins to the letters on the pies.

Unit 13 • Everyday Phonics Intervention Activities Grade K • ©2010 Newmark Learning, LLC

Overview Qq, Rr

Directions and Sample Answers for Activity Pages

Day 1	See "Model the Letter Q" below. Then ask students to raise their hands if their first or last name begins with the letter **Q**. Invite those students to write their names on chart paper. Circle the letter **Q** in each name. Tell students this is the letter **Q**. After, hand out the Day 1 activity page and read aloud the title and directions for the students.
Day 2	See "Model the Letter q" below. Then invite students to look for the letter **q** around the classroom—on books, posters, labels, etc. Have them share their findings with the class. After, hand out the Day 2 activity page and read aloud the title and directions for the students.
Day 3	See "Model the Letter R" below. Then ask students to raise their hands if their first or last name begins with the letter **R**. Invite those students to write their names on chart paper. Circle the letter **R** in each name. Tell students this is the letter **R**. After, hand out the Day 3 activity page and read aloud the title and directions for the students.
Day 4	See "Model the Letter r" below. Then invite students to look for the letter **r** inside books, magazines, and other materials. Check their findings to make sure they are correct. After, hand out the Day 4 activity page and read aloud the title and directions for the students.
Day 5	Read aloud the directions. Allow time for students to complete the task. Afterward, meet individually with students to discuss their results. Use their responses to plan further instruction and review.

Model the Letter Q

◆ Write the letter **Q** on the chalkboard. Tell students this is uppercase **Q**. Trace your finger over the letter **Q**, starting at the top, and **say:** *Q is circle around, lift, slant right at the bottom.*

Model the Letter q

◆ Write the letter **q** on the chalkboard. Tell students this is lowercase **q**. Trace your finger over the letter **q**, starting at the top, and **say:** *q is circle back around , push up, pull down.*

Model the Letter R

◆ Write the letter **R** on the chalkboard. Tell students this is uppercase **R**. Trace your finger over the letter **R**, starting at the top, and **say:** *R is pull down, lift, curve forward, slant right.*

Model the Letter r

◆ Write the letter **r** on the chalkboard. Tell students this is lowercase **r**. Trace your finger over the letter **r**, starting at the top, and **say:** *r is pull down, push up, curve forward.*

Mystery Letter

Ask students to color the letter Q spaces green and all the other letter spaces orange.

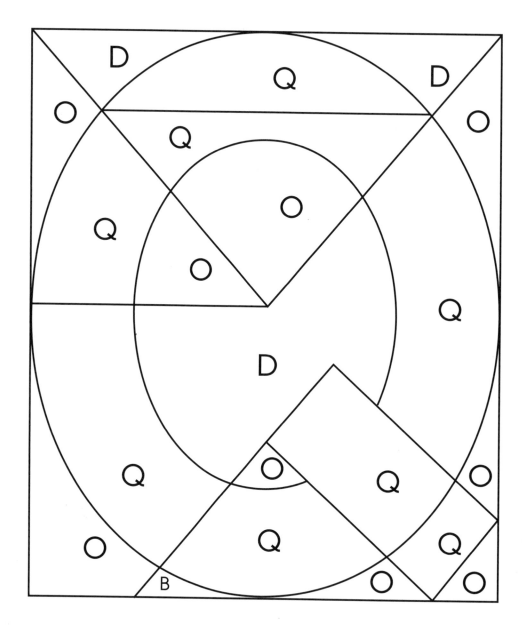

Trace and write.

Unit 14 • Everyday Phonics Intervention Activities Grade K • ©2010 Newmark Learning, LLC

Color the Quilt

Ask students to color the patches that have the letter *q* red. Color the patches with the letter *p* yellow. Color patches with the letter *Q* green. Color the patches with letter *P* blue.

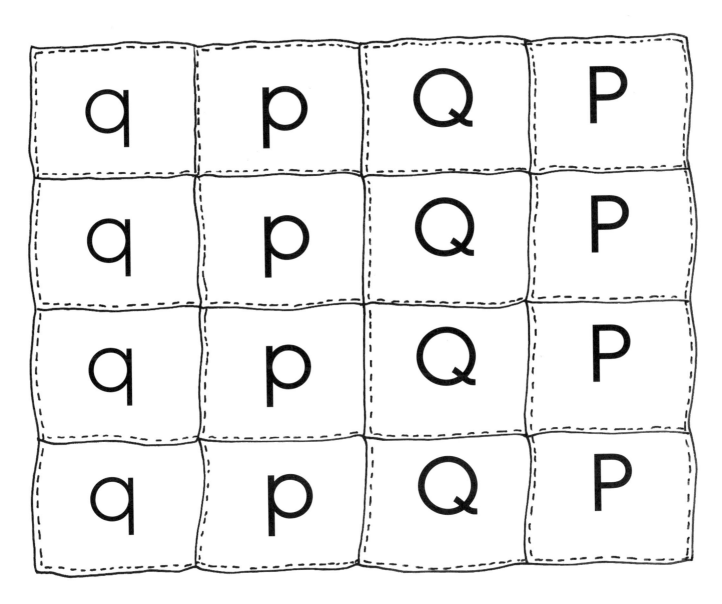

Trace and write.

Rock Hopping

Ask students to help Rabbit hop on the rocks to Rooster. Connect the rocks with the letter *R*.

Trace and write.

82   Unit 14 • Everyday Phonics Intervention Activities Grade K • ©2010 Newmark Learning, LLC

Roses Are Red

Ask students to color the letter *r* spaces red and the letter *R* spaces green.

Trace and write.

Name _____

Assessment

Ask students to look at each letter and draw lines from the raindrops to the matching umbrellas.

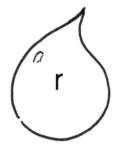

Overview   Ss, Tt

Directions and Sample Answers for Activity Pages

Day 1	See "Model the Letter S" below. Then ask students to raise their hands if their first or last name begins with the letter **S**. Invite those students to write their names on chart paper. Circle the letter **S** in each name. Tell students this is the letter **S**. After, hand out the Day 1 activity page and read aloud the title and directions for the students.
Day 2	See "Model the Letter s" below. Then invite students to look for the letter **s** around the classroom—on books, posters, labels, etc. Have them share their findings with the class. After, hand out the Day 2 activity page and read aloud the title and directions for the students.
Day 3	See "Model the Letter T" below. Then ask students to raise their hands if their first or last name begins with the letter **T**. Invite those students to write their names on chart paper. Circle the letter **T** in each name. Tell students this is the letter **T**. After, hand out the Day 3 activity page and read aloud the title and directions for the students.
Day 4	See "Model the Letter t" below. Then invite students to look for the letter **t** inside books, magazines, and other materials. Check their findings to make sure they are correct. After, hand out the Day 3 activity page and read aloud the title and directions for the students.
Day 5	Read aloud the directions. Allow time for students to complete the task. Afterward, meet individually with students to discuss their results. Use their responses to plan further instruction and review.

Model the Letter S

◆ Write the letter **S** on the chalkboard. Tell students this is uppercase **S**. Trace your finger over the letter **S**, starting at the top, and **say:** *S is curve back, curve forward.*

Model the Letter s

◆ Write the letter **s** on the chalkboard. Tell students this is lowercase **s**. Trace your finger over the letter **s**, starting at the top, and **say:** *s is curve back, curve forward.*

Model the Letter T

◆ Write the letter **T** on the chalkboard. Tell students this is uppercase **T**. Trace your finger over the letter **T**, starting at the top, and **say:** *T is pull down, cross at the top.*

Model the Letter t

◆ Write the letter **t** on the chalkboard. Tell students this is lowercase **t**. Trace your finger over the letter **t**, starting at the top, and **say:** *t is pull down, cross near the top.*

Snake Maze

Ask students to help Snake slither home. First tell them to connect all the *S* letters. Then color Snake and her home.

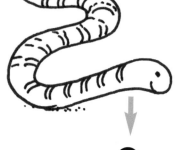

S	D	S	R	A
C	S	G	S	K
F	E	B	S	J
N	H	M	R	S

Trace and write.

Unit 15 • Everyday Phonics Intervention Activities Grade K • ©2010 Newmark Learning, LLC

Sock Match-Up

Ask students to cut out the letters at the bottom. Glue the socks with the letter *s* on the sock labeled *s*. Glue the socks with the letter *S* on the sock labeled *S*.

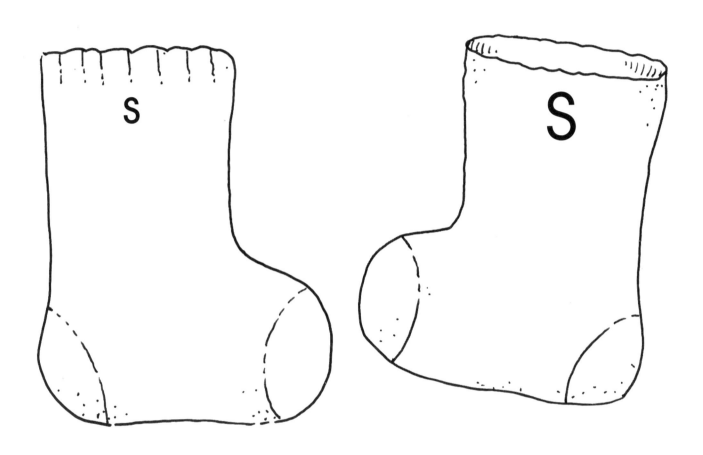

Trace and write.

Build a T

Ask students to color the pieces. Then help students cut the pieces out and glue them onto the paper to build a _T_.

Trace and write.

Name _____

Tic-Tac-Toe

Ask student pairs to cut out the letters. Then ask them to take turns putting their letters on the tic-tac-toe board. The first to get three in a row wins!

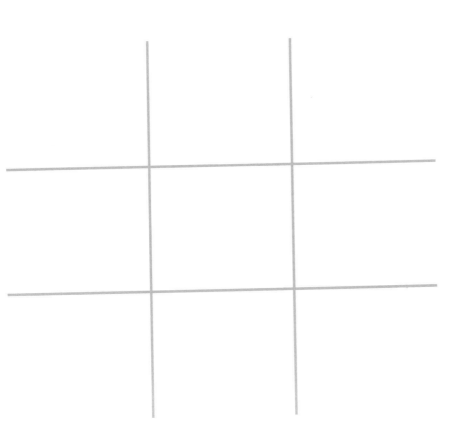

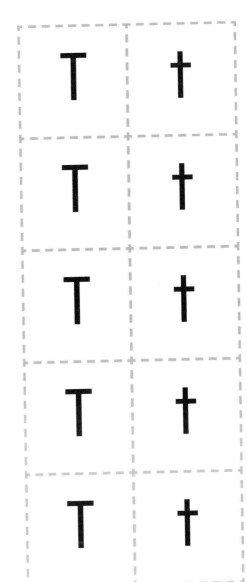

Trace and write.

Assessment

Ask students to name the letters in each row. Then ask them to circle the letters that match the first letter in each row.

S	C　S　s　C　S
S	C　O　s　s　S
T	T　F　T　t　J
t	f　t　j　T　t

Unit 15 • Everyday Phonics Intervention Activities Grade K • ©2010 Newmark Learning, LLC

Overview Uu, Vv

Directions and Sample Answers for Activity Pages

Day 1	See "Model the Letter U" below. Then ask students to raise their hands if their first or last name begins with the letter **U**. Invite those students to write their names on chart paper. Circle the letter **U** in each name. Tell students this is the letter **U**. After, hand out the Day 1 activity page and read aloud the title and directions for the students.
Day 2	See "Model the Letter u" below. Then invite students to look for the letter **u** around the classroom—on books, posters, labels, etc. Have them share their findings with the class. After, hand out the Day 2 activity page and read aloud the title and directions for the students.
Day 3	See "Model the Letter V" below. Then ask students to raise their hands if their first or last name begins with the letter **V**. Invite those students to write their names on chart paper. Circle the letter **V** in each name. Tell students this is the letter **V**. After, hand out the Day 3 activity page and read aloud the title and directions for the students.
Day 4	See "Model the Letter v" below. Then invite students to look for the letter **v** inside books, magazines, and other materials. Check their findings to make sure they are correct. After, hand out the Day 4 activity page and read aloud the title and directions for the students.
Day 5	Read aloud the directions. Allow time for students to complete the task. Afterward, meet individually with students to discuss their results. Use their responses to plan further instruction and review.

Model the Letter U

◆ Write the letter **U** on the chalkboard. Tell students this is uppercase **U**. Trace your finger over the letter **U**, starting at the top, and **say:** *U is pull down, curve forward, push up.*

Model the Letter u

◆ Write the letter **u** on the chalkboard. Tell students this is lowercase **u**. Trace your finger over the letter **u**, starting at the top, and **say:** *u is pull down, curve forward, push up, pull down.*

Model the Letter V

◆ Write the letter **V** on the chalkboard. Tell students this is uppercase **V**. Trace your finger over the letter **V**, starting at the top, and **say:** *V is slant right, slant up.*

Model the Letter v

◆ Write the letter **v** on the chalkboard. Tell students this is lowercase **v**. Trace your finger over the letter **v**, starting at the top, and **say:** *v is slant right, slant up.*

Name _____

Hidden Picture

Ask students to color each space with the letter *U* blue to reveal a magical creature.

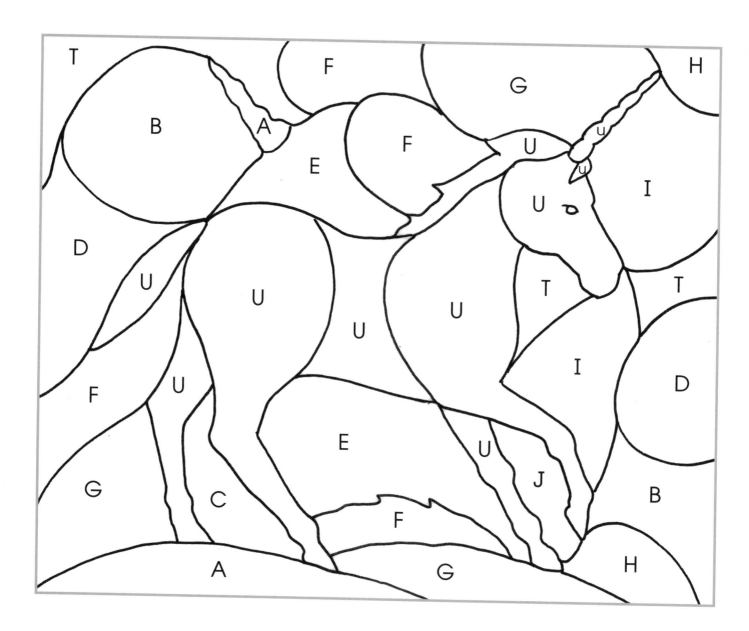

Trace and write.

Unit 16 • Everyday Phonics Intervention Activities Grade K • ©2010 Newmark Learning, LLC

Tic-Tac-Toe

Ask student pairs to cut out the letters. Then ask them to take turns putting their letters on the tic-tac-toe board. The first to get three in a row wins!

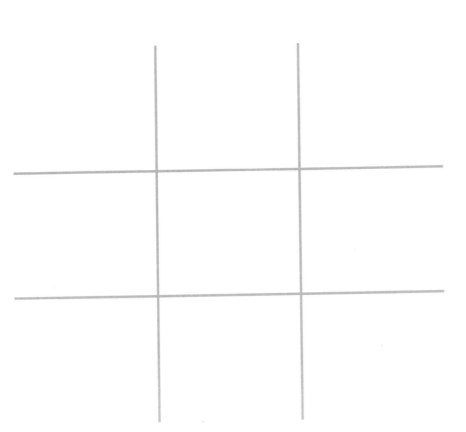

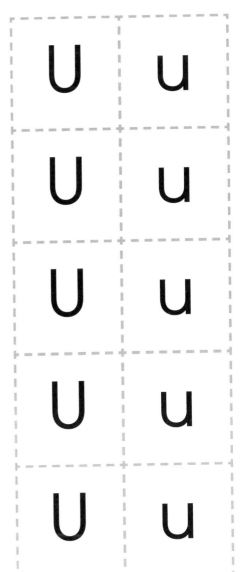

Trace and write.

Vegetable Soup

Ask students to cut out the vegetables with the letter *V* and glue them in the bowl of soup.

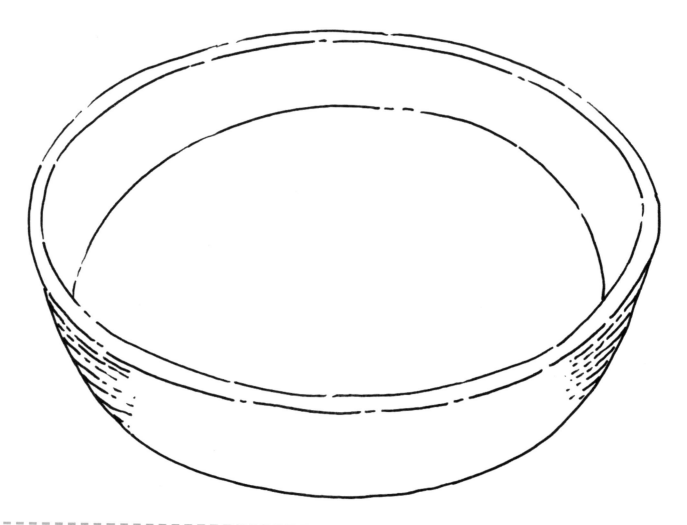

Trace and write.

V is for Vest

Ask students to color the vests with the letter *v* blue and the vests with the letter *V* red.

Trace and write.

Name _____

Assessment

Ask students to name the letters in each row. Then ask them to circle the letters that match the first letter in each row.

U	U V u V U
u	v v u U u
V	V U V V v
v	u v V v U

Overview Ww, Xx

Directions and Sample Answers for Activity Pages

Day 1	See "Model the Letter W" below. Then ask students to raise their hands if their first or last name begins with the letter **W**. Invite those students to write their names on chart paper. Circle the letter **W** in each name. Tell students this is the letter **W**. After, hand out the Day 1 activity page and read aloud the title and directions for the students.
Day 2	See "Model the Letter w" below. Then invite students to look for the letter **w** around the classroom—on books, posters, labels, etc. Have them share their findings with the class. After, hand out the Day 2 activity page and read aloud the title and directions for the students.
Day 3	See "Model the Letter X" below. Then ask students to raise their hands if their first or last name begins with the letter **X**. Invite those students to write their names on chart paper. Circle the letter **X** in each name. Tell students this is the letter **X**. After, hand out the Day 3 activity page and read aloud the title and directions for the students.
Day 4	See "Model the Letter x" below. Then invite students to look for the letter **x** inside books, magazines, and other materials. Check their findings to make sure they are correct. After, hand out the Day 4 activity page and read aloud the title and directions for the students.
Day 5	Read aloud the directions. Allow time for students to complete the task. Afterward, meet individually with students to discuss their results. Use their responses to plan further instruction and review.

Model the Letter W

◆ Write the letter **W** on the chalkboard. Tell students this is uppercase **W**. Trace your finger over the letter **W**, starting at the top, and **say:** *W is slant right, slant up, slant right, slant up.*

Model the Letter w

◆ Write the letter **w** on the chalkboard. Tell students this is lowercase **w**. Trace your finger over the letter **w**, starting at the top, and **say:** *w is slant right, slant up, slant right, slant up.*

Model the Letter X

◆ Write the letter **X** on the chalkboard. Tell students this is uppercase **X**. Trace your finger over the letter **X**, starting at the top, and **say:** *X is slant right, lift, slant left.*

Model the Letter x

◆ Write the letter **x** on the chalkboard. Tell students this is lowercase **x**. Trace your finger over the letter **x**, starting at the top, and **say:** *x is slant right, lift, slant left.*

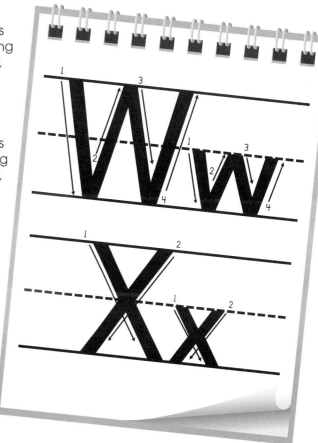

Wanda Walrus

Ask students to help Wanda Walrus find her way back home by following the letter *W* through the water.

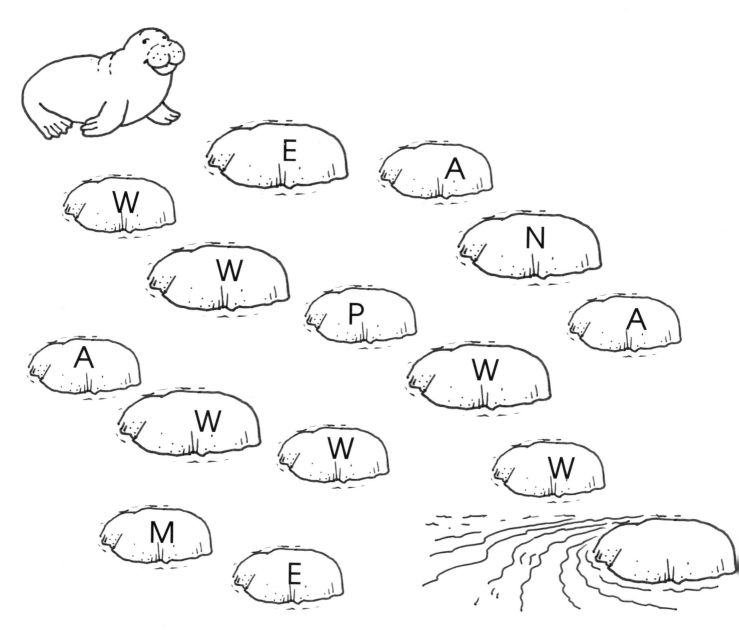

Trace and write.

Unit 17 • Everyday Phonics Intervention Activities Grade K • ©2010 Newmark Learning, LLC

Wishing Well

Ask students to look at the coins in the wishing well. Then ask them to color the coins with the letter *w* brown. Color the rest of the coins black.

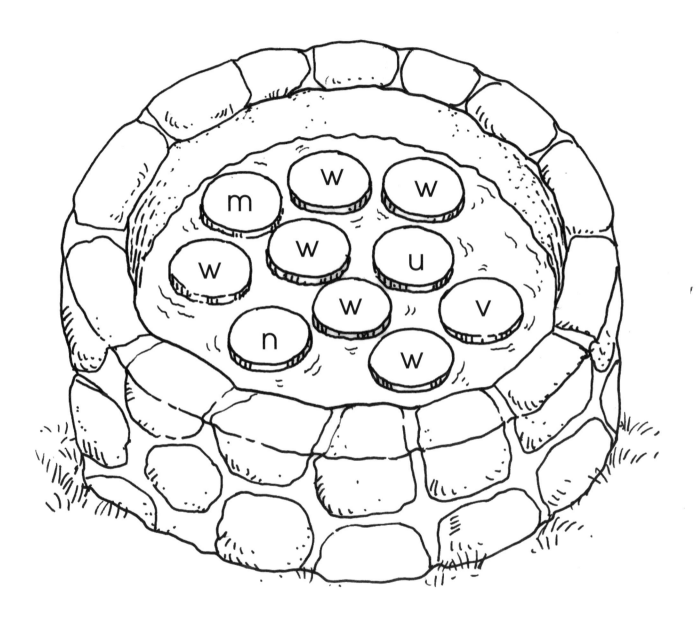

Trace and write.

W

Mystery Letter

Ask students to color each box with the letter *X* to find out.

X	M	m	N	X
N	X	M	X	X
N	n	X	M	m
N	X	M	X	m
X	M	n	m	X

Trace and write.

Tic-Tac-Toe

Ask student pairs to cut out the letters. Then ask them to take turns putting their letters on the tic-tac-toe board. The first to get three in a row wins!

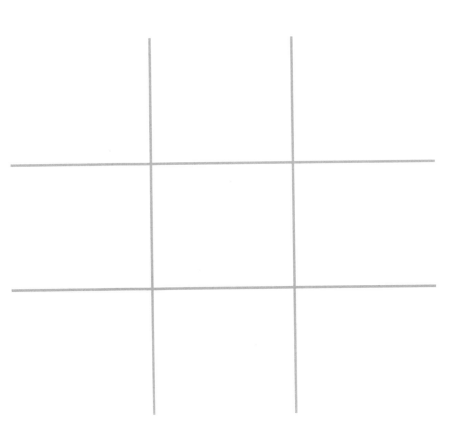

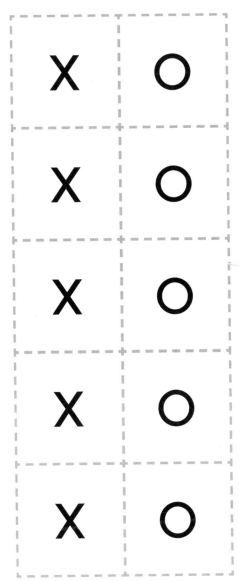

Trace and write.

Assessment

Ask students to draw lines to match the letters on the wagons with the letters on the wheels.

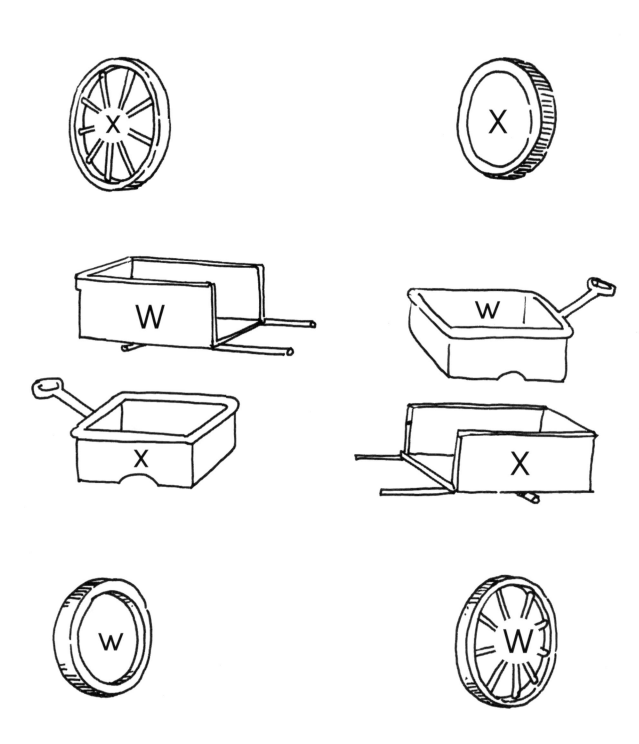

Unit 17 • Everyday Phonics Intervention Activities Grade K • ©2010 Newmark Learning, LLC

Overview Yy, Zz

Directions and Sample Answers for Activity Pages

Day 1	See "Model the Letter Y" below. Ask students to raise their hands if their first or last name begins with the letter **Y**. Invite those students to write their names on chart paper. Circle the letter **Y** in each name. Tell students this is the letter **Y**. After, hand out the Day 1 activity page and read aloud the title and directions for the students.
Day 2	See "Model the Letter y" below. Invite students to look for the letter **y** around the classroom—on books, posters, labels, etc. Have them share their findings with the class. After, hand out the Day 2 activity page and read aloud the title and directions for the students.
Day 3	See "Model the Letter Z" below. Ask students to raise their hands if their first or last name begins with the letter **Z**. Invite those students to write their names on chart paper. Circle the letter **Z** in each name. Tell students this is the letter **Z**. After, hand out the Day 3 activity page and read aloud the title and directions for the students.
Day 4	See "Model the Letter z" below. Invite students to look for the letter **z** inside books, magazines, and other materials. Check their findings to make sure they are correct. After, hand out the Day 4 activity page and read aloud the title and directions for the students.
Day 5	Read aloud the directions. Allow time for students to complete the task. Afterward, meet individually with students to discuss their results. Use their responses to plan further instruction and review.

Model the Letter Y

◆ Write the letter **Y** on the chalkboard. Tell students this is uppercase **Y**. Trace your finger over the letter **Y**, starting at the top, and **say: Y** *is slant right to the middle, slant left to the middle, pull down to the bottom.*

Model the Letter y

◆ Write the letter **y** on the chalkboard. Tell students this is lowercase **y**. Trace your finger over the letter **y**, starting at the top, and **say: y** *is slant right to the middle, lift, slant left to the bottom.*

Model the Letter Z

◆ Write the letter **Z** on the chalkboard. Tell students this is uppercase **Z**. Trace your finger over the letter **Z**, starting at the top, and **say: Z** *is slide right, slant left, slide right.*

Model the Letter z

◆ Write the letter **z** on the chalkboard. Tell students this is lowercase **z**. Trace your finger over the letter **z**, starting at the top, and **say: z** *is slide right, slant left, slide right.*

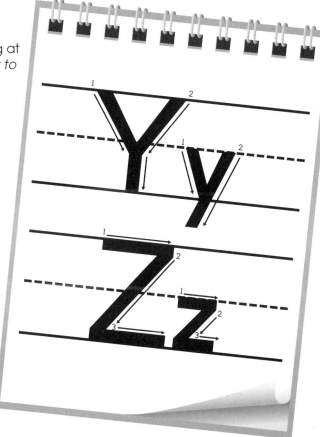

Y

Ask students to write *Y* in each box.

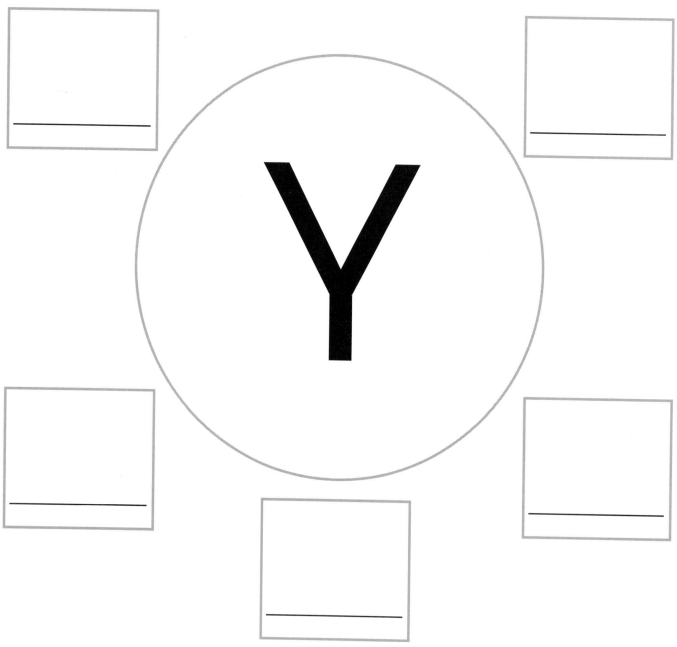

Trace and write.

Unit 18 • Everyday Phonics Intervention Activities Grade K • ©2010 Newmark Learning, LLC

Name _____

Mystery Picture

Ask students to color the spaces with the letter _y_ yellow and the spaces with letter _Y_ green.

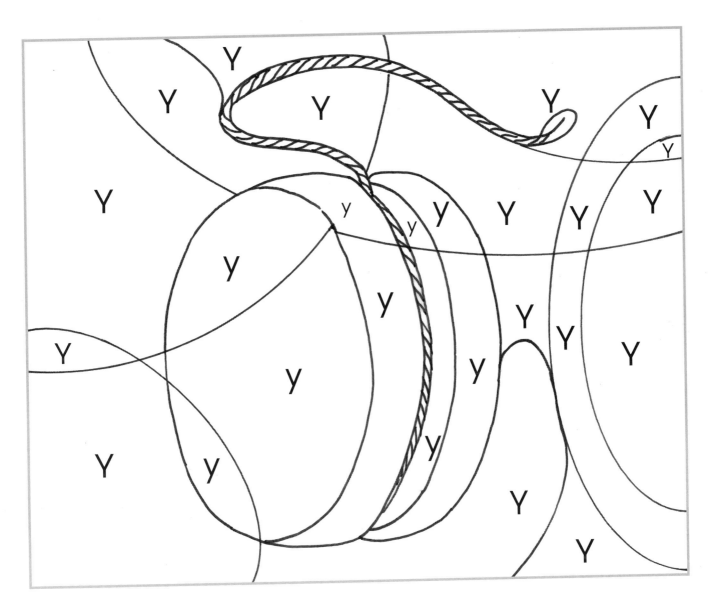

Trace and write.

Mystery Letter

Ask students to color each box with the letter Z to see the mystery letter.

Z	Z	Z	Z
C	B	Z	X
E	Z	M	A
Z	Z	Z	Z

Trace and write.

To the Zoo

Ask students to help Zebra to the zoo by circling and connecting all the *z* letters.

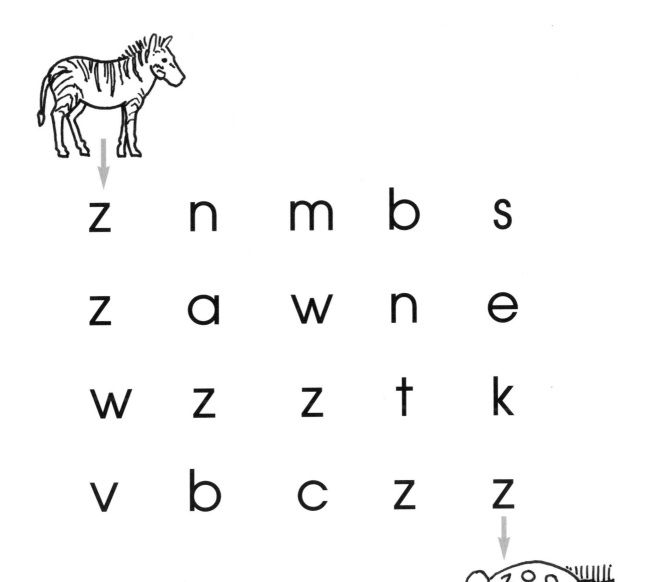

z n m b s

z a w n e

w z z t k

v b c z z

Trace and write.

Name _____

Assessment

Ask students to draw lines to match the letters on the jackets to the letters on the zippers.